BARK

LIFE LESSONS I LEARNED FROM DOGS

Other titles by J. Robert Ridpath

TLC for the body, mind and soul –
Addressing the underlying causes of chronic illness.

Belly fat and stress reduction (eBook)

Published by Health Synergy.
Copyright @2018 by J. Robert Ridpath.

All rights reserved. No part of this book may be reproduced or transmitted in any form or by any means, electronic or mechanical, including photocopying, recording, or by an information storage and retrieval system - except by a reviewer who may quote brief passages in a review to be printed in a magazine or newspaper – without permission in writing from the publisher.

The author and proof readers have used their best efforts in preparing this book and make no representations or warranties with respect to accuracy or completeness of the content. The purpose of this book is to educate about basic lifestyle changes. No individual should use the information in this book for self-diagnosis, treatment, or justification in accepting or declining any medical therapy for any health problem or disease. Any individual with a specific health problem or who is taking medications must first seek advice from their personal physician or healthcare provider before starting any nutritional, exercise or lifestyle program. The author shall have neither a liability, nor responsibility to any person or entity with respect to loss, damage, or injury caused or alleged to be caused directly or indirectly by the information contained in this book. We assume no responsibility for errors, inaccuracies, or omissions, or any inconsistency herein.

For information please contact:
Robert Ridpath
HealthSynergy.ca/contact
www.Healthsynergy.ca

Printed in Canada November 2018
Paperback ISBN 978-0-9865547-1-1
E-book ISBN 978-0-9865547-3-5

Cover and typesetting design: Health Synergy.

Attention corporations, universities, colleges, foundations and professional organizations:
Quality discounts are available on bulk purchases of this book for educational purposes.

Speaking engagements:
If you are interested in having Robert as a speaker, please contact Robert at Healthsynergy.ca/contact with your request.

Dedication

This book is dedicated to my daughters, Jenna and Jody. I hope the stories and lessons serve you well as you go through your life. And to my wife and all those wonderful dog owners (and animal owners) who know and value the bliss of having these amazing animals called dogs in their lives. May you live healthy and spirited lives, full of zest and "juice" with dogs at your side. Thank goodness for dogs!

Acknowledgements

I must say a huge thank you to all the veterinarians who shared so much with me over the years I worked in the animal hospitals. The clinical insights about animal welfare and life you shared has shaped me in profound ways. I'm so thankful you gave me a chance when others didn't. I have done my best to return the favour by producing this book for your animal loving owners.

Many thanks to Debbie Bateman for her editing guidance. It gave me some valuable insights and helped make this a better book for you. And, many thanks to those who proof read the first edition; I know it was far too meandering and long and thank you for your diligence, perseverance and feedback. I believe it made this book that much better.

As well, special thanks to my wife Heather for editing the many drafts of this book. It wouldn't be the same without her insights and input. Thank goodness for her patience with me.

Contents

Introduction 7

LESSON 1
Becoming Response-able........... 11

LESSON 2
Feeding the Body 26

LESSON 3
Attitude and Mindset 35

LESSON 4
Being Authentic and Real 57

LESSON 5
Simplify..................................... 74

LESSON 6
Social Connections 81

LESSON 7
The Game of Catch 87

LESSON 8
Presence 93

LESSON 9
Happiness 101

LESSON 10
Love 119

LESSON 11
The Life Cycle 132

LESSON 12
Gratitude and Letting it Go...... 141

Introduction

Welcome, I'm glad you found this book. I think there is some great material here for you. Who I am? My name is Robert and I'm a dog person.

I'm loyal, trustworthy, dependable, protective, fun, kind of simple and good natured. I love to be outside and socializing with others, playing and enjoying the day as well as the moment. I'm not too complicated in the ways I see and interact with the world. I love a good meal and to be challenged as I keep learning, growing and developing.

In the early 80's I worked in a busy animal hospital for six years. I was very fortunate that I was able to work with many, many dogs, cats, birds, skunks, ferrets, and even owls. I greatly appreciate them all with their uniqueness and special adaptations. I also worked with horses and was a lead hand in a riding stable. I'm so intrigued by the grandeur and majestic nature of horses. Their size still scares me a bit but I'm in awe of their strength, power and speed. I find they are such amazing creatures, especially with the unique bonding between rider and animal, and especially when in close union when the team moves as one and has "flow" and synergy. Riding through the woods on a warm day is absolutely amazing. I love and respect horses, but I'm a dog person.

I relate to dogs because of the unconditional love, always up to play attitude, good nature and the social wanting them and I strongly relate to and I would say need! Many have written about the special and unique bond that develops between dogs and their owners. This synergistic relationship goes back thousands of years. I've even learned that the modern dog, because of its selected breeding, would almost rather be with its human owner than with its own kind. We have bred and morphed this animal into the ultimate human companion and friend! And I love them.

Don't get me wrong, I love and appreciate cats for their stealth, hunting ability, agility and independent nature. Mother Nature has done a wonderful job of creating such a unique creature, but I can't fully relate to them. I just don't get the nocturnal thing or the snobby almost arrogant attitude. Sorry! I still have a place for them in my heart, but there won't be much about them in this book. I'm a dog person. And this book is about all the ways they've enhanced and bettered my life and the lessons I've learned from them.

Why am I dog person? I feel incredibly grateful that they have been a part of my life for so many years. It's not what you can do for a dog, rather, it's what can a dog do for you! They taught me many life lessons and helped shape me to be the person I am. They taught me to be kind, gentle, and caring. They taught me about "tough love", compassion, joy and happiness. And very importantly, they taught me about presence and enjoying the day as well as taking as much as possible from the day instead of just getting through it. Studying them I learned about the importance of social connections and engagement and how to find happiness within me so I can go about happily achieving as I enjoy the moment of the day.

Further, they helped teach me how to get in touch with my instincts and listen to my inner voice all of which were so important for helping me finding my own direction and happiness. This I believe has helped me become more real and authentic. Dogs taught me about the life cycle, love, friendships and how to be responsible. For this I feel deeply in debt to them. Yes indeed having dogs in my life has been a blessing. I'm gushing over with gratitude thus I wanted to give them credit and thanks for bettering my life and me. If you're reading this you most likely feel the same! I've learned so much from them that I want to give back to others and share some of the life lessons they taught me.

When they come into your life they steal your heart and when they go they tear it out. And in-between they stir us in every possible way. Dogs can help us to chill out, relax and laugh with their silly and sometimes outrageous and bazaar antics. If laughter is medicine for the soul, then dogs are great purveyors of this elixir.

When the student is ready, the teacher will appear. This is what I found with the dogs in my life. We will all get different lesson from the dogs in our lives depending on where we are in our personal growth and stage of life. I'm sure there will be common lessons we all get such as a deeper awareness of the life cycle, but I also think we will get unique lessons, just for us as we spend more time with them. It could be as simple as how they get us out to walk them in the parks and woods thus giving us a more acute awareness of the day, the weather, and the amazing seasonal changes. It could be that they introduce us to new fellow dog walkers who become friends and boost our socialization. Or it could be the sense of contentment and peace of mind we have as we pat them and appreciate how lucky we are to have them in our life.

I've tried to weave stories of the events leading to how the lessons were learned, how I applied them and how they impacted my life. I will also give you a few thoughts on how you could apply the lessons in your own life if you like.

Even though we had numerous family dogs when I was growing up it's when my own dogs came into my life at the age of 20 where their impact was most pronounced on my destiny. They helped changed the unhealthy direction my life had taken and helped steer me towards a much more positive and rewarding future. Thus I'm writing this book to express my gratitude and thanks to dogs that have been in my life and those dogs of the world. It's all good karma!

We have all had special people who impact our life in some unique way, thus I would like to give a great thanks to Dr. B.J. Beresford for giving me the opportunity to work with her at the animal clinics. As a twenty year old, grade 10 drop out she saw something in me that I couldn't see in myself. Her mentoring, guidance and patience to put up with my shenanigans allowed me to grow into the person I am today. Her life lessons I continue to use every day to keep me on the up and up. I'm even passing them on to my children.

I also need to give thanks to Dr. Mark Cole for inspiring and convincing me to go back to school and to university. As well as to Dr. Penny Rowland for giving me the opportunity to build my skills and confidence.

I also want to thank Kathy Duncan for giving me my own first dog, Lady. (My first "kid".) This life-altering event helped me grow from an obnoxious, irresponsible, self-centered, reckless teen into a responsible adult. I can't even fathom where I would be or how my life would be without this transformational moment in my life. I'm forever grateful and thankful for her kindness. She is a dog person!

I hope you can find a little strength, courage, inspiration and maybe even motivation from my experiences. I hope you laugh and I hope you cry. As well, my desire is that the experiences and lessons I learned from dogs and share in this book serve you well in your life going forward. Remember, you are not a human being, you are a human becoming! And dogs can help you with that evolution.

I wish you the best of health and spirits on your journey along the path of life. May you be blessed with a dog or two at your side.

Robert Ridpath

LESSON 1
Response-able

"Ghetto Child" isn't the most flattering and supportive name to be called but it's what many of the other kids called me. And I didn't like living in "Ghetto Village", which was a subsidized government housing development. The Ghetto name came from the street name, Grado. It's not a place I wanted to be, but life had different plans for me. I just had my twentieth birthday and life was about to get a whole lot more "fascinating" with a new dog in my life.

The summers in Toronto, the city of trees, were always hot and today was no different but being the end of August it was hot and stinking humid so my tee shirt was almost painted on my back with sweat as I walked. And of course when I stopped walking, poof, my whole body was instantly covered in dripping sweat from all my pores. I could taste the salt on my lips. It was even dripping off my forehead and down off the tip of my nose. Gross!

Suburbia can be boring for teenagers and Don Mills, being a newish development in Toronto in the 1970's was no different. From my point of view it was bland, void and lacking much character. It was "boring". As I had to walk everywhere I noticed the streets were all different but yet, they were the same. Simply rows of houses with small twig like trees out front, the basic little plot of green grass, a few basic hedges between the houses, very little landscaping, a few cars and bicycles and a fire hydrant every 25 houses or so. And of course they were all built close to the big highways so the parents could rush off to work in the downtown core.

There were large clusters of apartment building and rows and rows of townhouse developments. With so many living spaces in such a small area, there were a lot of kids. And, with so many restless kids and so little to do in a "boring" neighborhood it seemed trouble was always just around the corner.

As I walked the low dull whine from the 401 highway was getting louder so I knew her house was getting closer. I was walking to see Kathy, a girl I had being dating. We had since broken up and were still friends but in that awkward and weird kind of way after people breakup. She had invited me over to hangout… or so I thought.

It was my 20th birthday and Kathy had been acting "funny" for the last week or so. She insisted I come over for a visit. When she came to the door she had this big smile on and was almost giddy. My spider sense was tingling. Something's up! Then I heard the bark. It wasn't the bark I was used to. It wasn't Kathy's little dog Hoover's high pitch bark. What the hell was that? Kathy was now over the top giddy and very pleased with herself.

I noticed behind her a small, slight built, black lab looking puppy coming towards us as we stood at the front door. It barked again. "That's your birthday present Rob," she shouted at me almost in fits of laughter and glee. "Your mom and me have been working on getting you a dog for a while. We thought it would be a great present for you". My first thought was you have got to be frigging kidding! I started thinking, is this what I get as a replacement after a breakup with a broken heart, a frigging dog! I can't look after a dog! I don't want a dog! Oh NO! This is a mistake.

Little did I know this would be a transformational day for me. Having this puppy, whom we called Lady, come into my life would start a major correction in my life direction. It would start me towards a path I would never in a million years consider or even dream about. A life that I didn't think was possible for me. I cursed them for giving me this dog now, but I so much loved and appreciated them later. Little did I know life was going to get a bit more "interesting" with my next move in a few weeks to Ghetto Village.

The road to Ghetto village was a rough and bumpy downhill slide. A year or so earlier we were forced to move from the townhouse where we were living. My dad was going "crazy". His mental health had greatly deteriorated. His brain was messed up from the shock therapy and insulin coma's they put him in and the meds made him a zombie, a scary one at that. (The 70's weren't a good time for those with mental health issues.) He hadn't been working because of this state and he hadn't paying the bills.

My old red and rusty ten-speed bicycle came to a stop and I laid it down on the little hill out front of the townhouse. I was always hungry and had rushed home early from school to eat. There was a big white piece of paper on the door. It looked kind of like the eye charts at the doctor's office with the big letters at top and then getting progressively smaller as you read down the chart. I could only read the large font up top. I read the words "EVICTION NOTICE". As I got closer I could see the other words. Sheriff's office, blah blah blah. They didn't matter. I knew what had happened. I tried to open the door but it was bolted shut. They had removed my parents and we now weren't living here anymore. Where did my parents go? Where did my two younger brothers and older brother go? And where was my sister? Life was going to start getting more challenging for me. I had to find a place to live and find a job. I wouldn't see my father again for almost ten years.

I moved around to a few places over the next year but ended up at Ghetto Village in September 1980 just after my twentieth birthday with my mother and two younger brothers, Will and Peter. My older brother Tiff and sister Jane had been smart enough to get their own places a bit earlier.

Driving by from the road at first glance you might not think this place was so bad, they looked like many other townhouses in the area and the small cramped living spacers were actually ok, but it was the environment and the people living there that made this place a soul sucking hell hole for me.

Just like in the movies when the camera goes down a street filming in slow motion you can see beat up and run down old houses, cars, garbage and crap everywhere with people wearing tattered clothes sitting out front watching you and the world go by. That's what it was like for me.

The narrow streets with the packed townhouses were just meters from the busy and active train tracks. And we were definitely on the wrong side of them! The residences themselves were not very wide but instead they were built up with many floors. They had a deep red brick on the bottom floor and off white metal siding up top. The most distinguishing feature for me though was the cardinal iconic structure, the thick brownish metal railings that were everywhere. Out front, out back, around the edges of the driveways, around any green space, around the parking lots- it was everywhere! However, at about two feet high it did make for a convenient place to sit, have a drink and shoot the shit. And many took advantage of this.

Ghetto Village had character and it had drama. It was filled with a lot of shady and tough looking people. This place came alive in the afternoon when it seemed everyone woke up from their previous night's stupor. They would sit out front smoking, drinking, spouting off how the world had done them wrong and their tales of woe. Everyone had a story. The "poor me" victim mentality was rampant here. These people only seemed to be able to see the negative in their world and they loved to share it. The cops were "visiting" us a few times a day. Another weird thing, no one seemed to work here and if they were it was an "under the table" gig.

My two younger brothers, my mom, a younger family friend named Alistair, and I all lived here with all the other "losers and low lives"; the other alcoholics, drug addicts and down and outs. I hated living here. Interestingly enough, I never thought about the fact that these people probably didn't like living with me either!

Even though I seemed to fit right in with this "lively" crowd I despised these people and this place. It may have been that I saw too much of myself in them or that they were foreshadowing what was to come in my life. It didn't matter. I was deeply stirred to get the hell out of there. I've got to get out of here was a consistent thought. But how?

It's hard to understand but as I experienced, your environment shapes you. Living in such a negative environment can really pull you down. You can fight it and try to stay above it but the mindset and attitude of such a place slowly gets under your skin and you become part of it. As I learned later, this can go both ways though.

And I could feel it. I could feel this negative energy vortex sucking the life out of me. I could feel it slowly getting into my veins and then my brain. I could feel the suck of this place pulling me down and impacting my thoughts. You can fight it but its impact is relentless. I was starting to talk differently, act differently and be different. I couldn't resist what was happening to me. My one hope was, I had seen better. I knew there was a better place and I knew I had to break free and kill this poison that was in my soul. But how? How was I going to get out of this place? I had no resources, no money, no skills, no talent, no job, just a crappie attitude. And now I had the added responsibility of looking after a frigging dog.

Living with my younger brothers made me want to set an example of better character. I wanted them to be better than what I was. I thought I could somehow lead, teach and inspire them to be better than the surroundings we were in. To live up and into the people I could see them becoming. I saw potential in them. I somehow wanted to dig us out of this hell pit we were living in. I wondered sometimes how low could we go? How bad was this going to get? I knew it wasn't right for me. I knew in my heart there was something better. I could see how some of my friends had better lives, better families and how "normal" families interacted and functioned. Maybe I could use them as role models and inspiration to motivate me to get out of this place. Or maybe the drive to do something good for the dogs was the answer. This little back lab-terrier puppy name Lady was going to play a special role in my growth and development.

Becoming Response-able

A few months later I was learning the lesson that owning a dog can be expensive. I was told that Lady would have to be spayed so she didn't have puppies. I slammed the front door to the clinic hard and the "open" sign with the clinic hours rattled as I left. I was taking my frustrations out on the door. I was in a nasty, vile mood after leaving this vet's office. I wasn't happy about owning a "stupid" dog. No not me. I was used to doing what I wanted when I wanted. I didn't like being tied down. I had stuff to do. It was all about me. I was trying to work lots of hours to make some money, which was few and far between. And, as I didn't have much money I sure felt resentful and bitter spending the little I had on dog food. And now, the damn vet bills were a killer. That took away from the party fund. Damn dog! Why did they get me a dog?! I can't look after a dog. I'm not responsible. I don't want to be responsible. I don't want a frigging dog. Crap! Why did they do this to me!

Driving home in silence stewing about the money I had just dished out for the dog I started thinking about how I was going to manage and pay for these additional expenses. I really didn't want the dog at this point and I had the realization that I'm going to be "tied down" for a few years with it. What an anchor. Crap! I was feeling so resentful towards this dog. I even thought, how could I get rid of it, this damn animal burden?

Reflecting back, maybe it was the first hint of responsibility that hit me but I started to have a different understanding on how my parents might have felt. Maybe this is what they experienced once they decided to have kids. Resentful and bitter that these now five kids disrupted their lifestyle and drained the little money they had. They didn't seem to want to invest any time in us. Heck, they didn't even want to feed us. The cupboards were almost always empty. Good old Captain Crunch, Honey Comb and Carnation Instant Breakfast were the three meals a day staples in our home. (I loved the sugar.) And I'm sure the damn clothing and dentist bills were a killer on their finances. I don't think they wanted to be responsible. Damn kids!

In hindsight, it's interesting how cycles repeat. I could now see how this was happening in me based on my childhood experiences. And I wondered, how did I end up here? What's wrong with me? Why had this happened to me? Hindsight is always very clear and looking back this "sudden" bad luck had been brewing for a long time. I would even say even since I was just a kid when we moved to Toronto in 1968.

Nighttime is when the excitement and action happened. This is when the primal instincts of a pack kicked in and boldness flowed forth. This is when thrills and adrenalin flowed, when one could feel alive after a chase. Shit happened! From the age of nine in the late 60's, the summer nights were incredible. I would stay out all night roaming the suburban neighborhood with a gang of four or five. I told my parents I was staying over at my buddy Mark's house and he told his parents the same. We never went there and just stayed out all night. We all did this. My parents never inquired more. They never asked what we did or where we were. There was a total disconnect, probably because they were dealing with their own issues. My dad was going crazy with a mental illness and the booze kept them in depression and denial. They never invested the time to "train" us. In hindsight I can't even imagine all the horrific stress and dysfunction that filled our house. I was never there.

My early teen years were full of upheaval and rebellion. I was only 13 but things had already escalated out of control. There was lots of booze, drugs, crazy stupid shenanigans, pranks, petty crime and highly reckless antics. So many dumb and irresponsible things I can't even begin to mention them all. I thought I was cool with my long blonde hair, faded Levis jean jacket, and jeans, the white Adidas Rom leather shoes and big attitude, but in reality, I was just a lost fool being blown around by the winds of change.

These antics attracted trouble with the law. I spent little time at school and way too much time in juvenile court. After fifteen or so visits the judge who now knew me by sight and name decided to put a stop to things for a while. "You're on a bad path Mr. Ridpath" he boldly stated at my last "visit". "You need to become more responsible". I ended up in a juvenile boy's detention home, or "kiddy jail" as my brother liked to call it, for over a year. I later heard the rhyme that time in the clink gives you time to think.

Looking back I realized that structure was good; it helped in some ways, but it didn't seem to help change the direction I was headed. It didn't change my mindset or my beliefs or my crappy attitude. Now I rode motorcycles, stayed out late into the night partying, did what I wanted when I wanted and really didn't give two hoots about others, their wants or needs. I was impulse driven. Rules were for others. I did my own thing. Have you heard the old saying, hire a teenager while they still know it all? I was still a teenager and I thought I knew it all. I had little money and little education but man I made up for it with lots of big attitude. You know, that mouthy know it all crap that spews out of some, I had lots of it. With this mindset I didn't bother listening to "dumb" old people, what did they know any ways. I wasn't good in school and since I knew it all, I was uncoachable. Responsibility wasn't in my vocabulary. The rut was getting deeper as I got older. DAMN! Why did they get me a frigging dog!

So here I was, now twenty years old with a dog I didn't want and having to grow up and be responsible to take care of her. Lady was part terrier and part black lab with a wonderful rich dark black coat with an incredible shine like it had just been oiled. Her eyes were deep brown with soft velvet ears that flapped over the side of her head. She grew to be about 35 pounds and was so fast, agile, almost wiry, and incredibly athletic. Her spirit was kind, gentle and forgiving. She was also a bit timid and shy. And man oh man, this dog was smart. The contrast of her character to mine broke me down quickly. Her actions and behaviour were in such contrast to mine, it made me realize how much of a jerk I was and could be. I couldn't be mad or angry around her. If I was, she would retreat and pull back. I didn't want a dog but for some reason I wanted her to like me and listen to me so I had to be gentle and patient (not my strengths) with her. And somehow this dog made me laugh and smile with her playful antics and games. She got me engaged in life in a new way, in the outdoors and in learning. Weird.

I knew nothing about dogs so I went to the local library to get a few books on how to look after them (no internet in 1980). I came across a book on dog field trials. Wow, this grabbed my attention. A dog could actually "listen" and understand a person's hand signals, follow their commands and do some of this really cool stuff! I wanted to know more about this. I got more books, did more reading and spent lots and lots of time outside in the woods building my communication skills and relationship with this awesome little dog. I took her to the public school kids play ground and taught her to climb slides, jump over or shimmy under benches, how to climb trees, jump hoops and the difference between balls, sticks and Frisbees. I took her on the busses, streetcars and the subway in Toronto. She got tons of different life exposures. This was her culturing. And in fact, this was my therapy. Little did I know this was a transformational turning point in my life.

I decided Lady needed a friend to keep her company when I was away working at a new job so we started looking for one. Mom's arms were full of the grocery bags and there were two strange teenage boys with her. "I found a dog" she happily shared. You found a dog? Was my first response. Where? She began to share how when she was leaving the mall with all the groceries she saw these two boys with a puppy in a box. She stopped to pat and see the puppy. One of the boys then asked if she wanted it? She replied, "Well my son is looking for a dog. Tell you what, if you give me a ride home I will check with him to see." Next thing we know, Mom's coming in with the groceries and a puppy.

This new puppy seemed wild and out of control, kind of like how I was, so we called her Casy. She was a yellow lab German Shepherd cross. She looked like a Shepherd but had the yellow fur colour of the lab, a deep black snout with patches of white on her chest and tail. And like Lady, deep brown eyes. She also had big pointy ears that stood straight up making her always look alert. These ears would make Spock envious. Casey also took very well to training. With Lady as a model and mentor and with all the time my two younger brothers and I spent with the dogs they were becoming very well behaved and responded very well to voice and hand commands. We were training them well.

It didn't happen overnight, it was much more subtle. I didn't even know it was happening. Slowly I started shifting my focus away from me to them. It was a weird sensation for my ego shifting from "what about me" and all the selfishness and self-centeredness to them and their needs. It was a strange feeling becoming other focused and less absorbed in my own problems and issues. I had these strong nurturing feels. I was actually starting to care about these dogs at a deeper level.

The library was a great place for me. I spent more and more time reading, studying and then implementing the teachings and strategies I learned from the books with the dogs, who I affectionately started calling my "kids". A strange new feeling came over me; I wanted to raise good kids. Furthermore, I was accepting the idea of being committed to them for the long haul. They were keepers and I was a lifer!

And, another new thought came to me and this one threw me off guard; I started planning for the future, not just living for the day. I started feeling obligated to act and behave more grown up and correct (read this as "mature and responsible"). I became more aware of my actions and how others perceived and interacted with me. I felt others were watching me to see how I did. (Try taking a large and medium size dog on a busy bus during rush hour and see how many people look at you!) I felt like I had to act as a role model. I had to act responsible with these animals. I didn't want to be known as one of those "asshole dog owners" or trouble. I had to step up into this new role that made me feel very awkward, as I didn't know what was expected of me or how to act. The dogs helped me with this.

Funny enough, I felt so proud when people would comment and state how well behaved and trained the dogs were. Ah, I was a proud poppa. And I wanted more! I took responsibility for their good behaviour; that was nice, but I also had to take responsibility for their messes and the trouble they got into. I accepted full responsibility for both their good and bad actions. I didn't make excuses or blame others for their behaviour or actions. It was all on my shoulders. I stood tall and proud with that feeling. I had never had these feeling before and this was so strange for me to experience.

Stepping Up - Doing What Has To Be Done
It was a gross mess, kind of foamy, full of chunks and it was still warm. I could see all the chunks of dog food, I could see chunks of fur and it seemed, I could see half the pine tree Casy had eaten out back. It smelt like hell, was oozy and warm as I scooped it up with paper towels. You know what happens, it always squishes out the sides and drips back onto the floor or your hand. Just looking at it from this point blank distance made my stomach churn. I almost added to the pile. And this lovely "stew" wasn't on the cement floor or even the wood floor where it would be easier to clean up. No, Casy liked us too much for that. She gave us her best. This lovely pile was delivered on the carpet in the TV room for all to enjoy. I hated this frigging dog sometimes.

But I did what had to be done, that which every dog owner has done many, many times, I cleaned up the barf. I got part of that mess on my hands, it was gross but I cleaned it up. The first few times when things like this happened, I had the immature, self-centered response of a young frustrated male; I went and yelled at the dog and scolded her. Sometimes I would even grab her by the neck and shake her, yelling "bad dog". I was such a jerk. But I was changing. This time I went and comforted her by rubbed her belly speaking softly and reassuring her that things would be ok. We snuggled!

This wasn't the first time or the last time I did something I really didn't want to do or I wasn't in the mood to do. I didn't "feel" like cleaning up this barf but it had to be done. So I did it. This applied to cleaning up dog poop outside on our walks or when they left one in the house, or even in the car! This applied to when I had to get up early to take them out for a walk (teenagers love to sleep in) or when I had to take them out in a nasty rainstorms or a super cold frosty day, or even when I had to come home early at night, (I couldn't stay out all night parting anymore). I came home and took them out. I didn't want to, I wasn't in the mood, and I didn't feel like it. I was even resentful; but I did it because it was the right thing to do. I was putting their needs before mine. What a concept.

These were just small tiny steps that I consistently applied. And a weird thing started to happen. I started liking the feeling of winning over my inertia and emotions. I liked pushing though my moods or feelings. It was empowering. Each time I choose to act when I didn't feel like it, or when I wasn't in the mood it was building my internal will power muscle. It was building my inner strength, my grit and power. I was becoming stronger and I found it easier to overcome problems (aka – challenges). Things didn't stop me the way they did before. I didn't give up so easy. I had this new confidence and self-trust. I could take on bigger challenges or projects. If I said I was going to do something I did. Stuff started to happen. Cool! I was slowly morphing into a different person with a new deeper character. I was becoming "response-able". I was able to somewhat shape my life in the direction I wanted. This was empowering.

In weight lifting and body building you will often hear the term "body sculpting". You can do extra training on one area of your body to make it bigger, to add shape or definition and to add more overall symmetry to your look. Doing things I didn't want to do, and didn't feel like doing, was in hindsight "character sculpting".

Doing all these smaller tasks were shaping me, building me in new ways and reprograming my negative attitude and mindset. I was saying goodbye and closing the chapter on this ugly part of my life. It was time to let it go and move on. I didn't know it at the time but I was in the process of developing a new vision of my future. It was a blank page and I was writing the next chapter of my life with the vision of how I would live into it. I could make stuff happen. Whoa!

But it was no cake walk. I was always fighting and pushing back against the enemy. Building the internal strength and the internal motivation, as well as developing a big WHY was key to overcoming the enemy of inertia, of procrastination and fighting back against the killers of bad mood, poor attitude, laziness, self-doubt and lack of self-worth. You may have also had to fight these enemies of progress and forward progression. They're incredibly persistent and tenacious and just keep coming at us. I've found the battle has never ended.

Earlier in my life I would never have done things to improve myself. I wouldn't invest in my "self-care". I sure didn't have self-love. I think that with so many years of people saying I was "trouble", a druggie, looser, bum and that I was voted "most likely to end up in jail" by my high school peers, I was starting to believe them.

I didn't think too highly of myself and I didn't think I was worthy of "self-care". After all, if my parents valued us they would have spent time with us, fed us and showed some sort of interest in what we did, wouldn't they? That wasn't the case so I assumed we weren't of value to them. If they didn't love us, how could we love ourselves? The ripple effect of mental illness is wide.

It was becoming a bigger problem. I was having motivation challenges with doing anything to improve myself. Why should I, I felt I wasn't worth it. However, sometimes I could find strength by doing things for others and in this case, it was my dogs. I found it was easier to do things for them if I knew it would help them grow, learn or give them enjoyment. When times were tough I gave up on myself but I didn't give up on my dogs. And they didn't give up on me. They must have believed in me when I didn't. Doing things for them actually helped pull me through these tough times.

Inspiration comes from the most unlikely of places. I'm not sure when the thought came to be but I had this idea that I wanted to help and work more with dogs; dogs that may have been hurt or injured or mistreated. I wasn't too keen on people as it seemed "dumb people" do dumb things to themselves and their dogs. I didn't want to spend my time with them. This is when I decided to apply for work at an animal hospital. Heck, I also had the thought I could save on my vet bills if I did.

The motorcycle dealership I went to was way out in Scarborough, which in the early 80's it was the "boonies". Not much was out that way. And just beside the dealership there was an animal hospital. I had seen this particular clinic for years. It had a big sign with a blue cross on it out front with the words "Animal Hospital" on it. There were large windows on either side where I could sometimes get a quick glimpse into the treatment or surgery rooms. It looked official and there was always a nice little white Porsche 944 parked out front. It intrigued me so I applied. I wasn't the smartest tool in the shed (I had to lie about my schooling as at age 20 as I had only finished grade 9) but I knew I could work hard and was now very passionate about my vision. I had no skills but I did get a position with them! It didn't pay, it was a volunteer position, but I was working at a vet clinic getting experience and helping make a difference in these animals that needed help!

Do you ever look back on situations or experiences and wonder about them, why they unfolded a particular way or why you did or didn't do something? This is one of them for me. I'm not sure why this clinic director and lead vet liked me. She sure intimidated the hell out of me with her refined mannerisms, confident personality, great people skills, patience, surgical skills and white sports car, but we seemed to work well together.

My timing was always right when it came to surgery time thus I was able to watch many hundreds of surgeries as the days and months went by. Blood didn't bother me. Neither did intestines, guts, maggot-infected wounds, or smashed jaws with broken teeth, tumors or any of that. My incredible curiosity and intrigue overcame any grossness or squeamish thoughts or feelings. Most of all, I loved to watch the bone surgery repairs. A little voice inside my head used to say "I could do this. This is what I want to do. I would be good at this. I could help these dogs. I could make a difference in their life". These thoughts were quickly squashed by my internal voice reminding me of my past, my troubles, my lack of skills, my lack of resources and pedigree. Who was I to think I could do these things. No one in my family history did these things. It just wasn't in the cards for me. All the labels others had used to define me I was now using to define myself. What a stifling anchor that I didn't even know was holding me back.

Earning Respect By Becoming Responsible

It was a nasty break. The leg had been run over and the long leg bone, the femur, was crushed and in many pieces. Dr. Beresford, or Bejai as we all called her, was stumped with how to repair this particular nasty break. It was bashed and broken into many small fragments and splinters and I think a few pieces were even missing! This woman had strong flexible fingers and incredible patience. She kept trying to wire the fragments together around the bone and each time it would implode in on itself. She would do this again and again trying a new combination to make it work. She just didn't give up. Here was a master clinician, an expert surgeon with tons of experience. If she was having a challenge this must be an unsolvable issue. I was usually very quiet and didn't talk or comment. What did I know? I was just this down and out kid. This time I just couldn't help myself. I knew how to solve this problem.

The words just blurted out of me. I suggested she drive a pin down the femur shaft and use it as an internal support lattice so the fragments don't fold in on themselves. Hmmm. She didn't look impressed with my thought and continued to try her way. Finally after a few hours of trying, in frustration and as a last resort she decided to give my idea a shot. She drove a pin down the shaft of the femur and then simply placed the pieces around it and wired them securely around the pin. Easy! When she inquired how I knew how to do this I matter of fact stated it was just like fixing a broken frame on a motorcycle. "You put a reinforcing support bar inside the two ends of the frame and weld a cover or surrounding support piece outside. Carpentry is carpentry except your nitrogen driven stainless steel drill cost two thousand dollars. My Black and Decker drill cost twenty bucks!" Our relationship changed after this. I felt a new level of respect from her towards me. A respect I had never felt from an adult before. What a lucky break for me!

Having surgery is the closest you or an animal will ever come to death. Monitoring and looking after an animal during these procedures is a life or death situation. It's a BIG responsibility and I was doing this. I had earned some trust and respect from these people. I felt great. My inner voice whispered a thought in my ear as I was falling asleep; maybe I could contribute something of value here! Maybe I can make a difference.

Thoughts were jumping in and out of my head. I was starting to formulate in my mind what I wanted to do with my life. I wanted to do small animal orthopedic surgery. This is who I would become. Then I had these thoughts; how should I dress? How should I act? What car should I drive? (I liked the sports car the vet drove.) She seemed successful. She dressed well, spoke with a calm, gentle and confident voice, went to lots of seminars to build her skills, was physically active and seemed to be well put together (and she had the sports car). Maybe if I do what she does, maybe if I act like she does, maybe if I learned what she knows, maybe I could become like her and have the success that goes with it? The realization hit me. The real question was; who would I have to become in character, in action and temperament to have the success I was thinking about? I later learned that the great master of personal growth, Jim Rohn stated, "Success is something you attract by the person you become". People were having trust in me. I was becoming responsible. I was on the road to success.

The big life-changing lesson I received from my dogs was that of responsibility and becoming response-able. How trust and respect are earned through both small consistent actions and hard work. It's not just simply given out because of entitlement or any old reason. You don't just get trust and respect for showing up, it's your actions that prove it. You have to earn it. You have to become response-able.

With dogs you aren't just given respect or trust. You have to earn it with your behaviour and actions. Dogs know who the nice people are. They also know who the jerks are. And funny enough, they stay away from them! If you're mean or grumpy they know it and stay way. If you're kind, gentle and friendly they gladly come over to say hi and get patted.

A big aha for me was understanding that putting others needs and wants ahead of mine contributes to one becoming "response-able". And shifting my thoughts from me to we helped build interactions that synergized and lead to outcomes I couldn't fathom of achieving by myself. Further, shifting your mindset from what can I get to what can I give and contribute is so rewarding and fulfilling. Helping dogs or others build their skills and achieve new things is so very rewarding for me.

I also discovered that becoming "response-able" and taking action when you don't feel like it or when you aren't in the mood is a vital key mindset on the road to success that enriches your life and opens up so many more opportunities. It makes you happier with a deeper sense of fulfillment and satisfaction with your life. It allows you to break away from a situation you're not happy with, so that you can add a new level of control to your life. You can guide the ship anyway you want. It builds the all-important confidence and self-trust we all need. It's very empowering. Amazing!

I'm not gifted athletically or academically. I grew up in dysfunctional family with mental illness, I had many troubles with the law and with substance abuse, and I didn't have a support system to help guide me. However, because of this key lesson I learned from dogs, I became response-able. For some reason bad things had kept happening to me. I now wanted good things to happen to me.

I became a seeker of tools, tips, resources; anything that would give me a break or advantage to help make up for my lack of talent and expertise. I bought books, went to workshops and seminars so I could learn some new ways and insights to do things. I changed my social circle and "friends" to get away from their influence. I realized that I needed to get as much help as possible.

Please believe me when I say, you don't have to be that smart, you don't need special contacts, you don't need to be that talented or have all the experience, or formal education, and you don't need to be the best looking. You just have to decide to become response-able and take action. I didn't have some big fancy plan or vision. I just planned to start and did. I did it for my dogs.

It is so easy to get overwhelmed with all that you have to do or could do. And yes there is so much you don't know and haven't figured out yet. So, here is the key, don't let the things you can't do or don't know stop you from doing the things you can do, the small simple things you can act on today. Just start taking action. You don't have to know all the steps or the exact sequence of things to do. I took tiny little steps to just nudge myself forward. That's all. Ask others for help and guidance. They will love to help you in the ways they can. Take action, get some movement and build momentum. Don't over think things. Thought before action is good. Action with intention is better!

I'm not sure what you would have done, but if I had to go back and do things all over again, I don't think I would ask for it to be easier. I wouldn't change things. The struggles and challenges I encountered because of my dogs helped shape me to be the response-able person who I am today. I've learned how to become bigger than my problems. This is something I'm very thankful for. I often reflect on how having dogs shaped my life. I also share with our children about dogs and their importance in my life. How lucky are we to have these amazing creatures in our life! Food for thought.

LESSON 2
Feeding the Body

The morning was brisker and there was dew on all the grass and plants. I even noticed the sun was rising later. I had to wear a sweater to cut the chill on the twenty-minute walk to my new place of learning. Eight years old and I was starting grade three. This was my first day at the new school, Three Valleys Public School, in the fall of '68. Being kind of a quiet and shy kid I was scared. The unknown is always scary and this big new school, with all the new kids, made me very apprehensive. I wasn't used to all the other kids. We moved to Toronto from a very small town called Lindsay just a week or so earlier on my eighth birthday. There we had lived outside of town with not too much interaction with other families or kids. I didn't want to go to school. I stared at the lines on the sidewalk as I shuffled my way along alone, worrying the worst, no one will like me. I'd have no friends. I wondered what my teacher and the class would be like.

The sounds of the springs had that characteristic squeak as you come down from a big jump. The ceiling was overly tall in this room, the windows were big and bright and there were the classic alphabet letters all around the top of the chalkboards, with pictures of puppies, horses, birds and other animals posted up. There was a large oak teacher's desk and a few of the small student desks, the ones you slip into from the side. And all I can think about is "I want to hit the roof". Grade three was turning out to be ok.

"Ok Robbie, what is this word?" the teacher would say as she flashed the card to me as I was jumping up and down on this trampoline. Boat, train, dog, horse…and so on I would answer. This was the best class of the day in grade three, other than gym. At the time, I never knew why my younger brother and I got to have all this fun. The other kids had to stay in class. I guess it was because we were "special" and good at jumping! I found out later that we were labeled "slow learners" and that this was some extra TLC to help us learn. The teachers were concerned, as I was also getting into fights everyday during recess or during the lunch breaks. Apparently, the trampoline was to help address my hyperactivity so I was calmer and could learn better.

In reflection, I find it interesting that we had all kinds of tests and evaluations. We even went to the fancy-dancy newly opened Clark Institute of Psychiatry in downtown Toronto for counseling because we were "slow learners" and had "family issues" yet no one ever asked us what we were eating! Now as an adult who studies nutritional biochemistry and nutrition I find this mind blowing. At the time, if they had asked I would have told them.

You see, there wasn't much money or food at our house and I never wanted to go home so I didn't eat there much. However, following my older brother's lead, I got a paper route, which was very common in the late sixties and seventies, and I used my paper money to buy food and snacks. Being just a small kid I didn't know what food was best. And I sure didn't know about the four food groups! I was driven by taste and energy output. It was normal for me to have four, five or more Cokes each day. I lived on Hickory Sticks, Joe Louis, Twinkies, popsicles, chocolate milk, Three Musketeer bars and caramels. Life was good. But as you may have guessed, after a few years of eating junk food I was turning into a little Buddha. Back then kids didn't get fat; they were called "Husky". I even had jeans that were called Husky!

Ten-year-old kids don't always make the best choices. I didn't know squat about the food groups, the food guides or veggies. Green smoothies weren't in vogue. All I knew is that I felt energized when I was eating this type food. I wanted to feel better and sugar and caffeine made me feel better so that's the food I ate. This also had the secondary effect of rotting away many of my teeth. How is it that dogs fit into this story? With my dogs, animals I greatly cared about, I didn't want to apply this same "strategy" to them. I wanted to make sure they did better than me. I was in for more life lessons and a new direction in my life.

Casy had a unique digestive issue in that she didn't absorb fats very well. She couldn't get enough calories and thus stayed skinny as a rake with her ribs prominently showing, and her coat was dry and lifeless. But the worst part was the chronic diarrhea. Gross! I tried a few things (read this as "guessed at") that I thought would help, but they didn't. There was no Internet and no "Doctor Google" in 1980 and there were no medical books at the library. Lucky for Casy and me though, I was volunteering at an Animal Hospital and they had medical books and lots of super smart people. I spent a lot of time reading, asking many, many questions and trying different diets and foods with Casy with little initial impact. It wasn't until I introduced a special food for intestinal and digestive health that things shifted in the right direction. The diarrhea stopped, she gained weight, her coat got thicker and shiny and she took better to the training. And most interestingly, her behaviour dramatically changed. It was so amazing and overwhelming to me that she was healing and acting so much better. I wondered if this would happen in humans.

Seeing such dramatic changes in my dog's health made me start a new tangent in my learning and taught me profound lessons on the importance of nutrition on health. I was curious to see if this would help me. I had suffered from chronic knee and joint pain my whole life. The doctors called it juvenile rheumatoid arthritis (an autoimmune disease) and it may have been caused by blood transfusions I had at birth. I was born as a "blue baby". Blue babies are those that need blood transfusions at birth due to incompatible blood proteins with the mother. They are blue because their blood can't carry oxygen, which makes the blood red and thus the blood stays blue. I was a blue baby as were my other brothers. In 1960 they didn't screen the blood the way they do today. I'm sure I got someone's funky blood that reacted with my immune system.

Over the years I tried so many different food plans, diets, and supplements it would make your head spin; wheat germ oil with raw eggs, ginger and kelp were staples for a few years. I ate cans and cans of tuna, more carrots than Bugs Bunny, and so many other things. I went to our family doctor and specialist. They were adamant that food had no bearing on my "disease", it was genetic. Finally after years of experimenting with different foods and eliminating others, one week by chance I was able to pinpoint the major food causing my knee pain… milk! By removing milk*, in less than two weeks, two decades of chronic pain and suffering was gone! GONE! It was such an eye opening and liberating experience. I knew there was a lot more here that I needed to understand. This started my life long (almost four decades now) deep interest in how nutrition affects the body, the brain and behaviour. All because my dog was skinny and had chronic diarrhea. Thank god for dogs!

I find it interesting, sad, as well as frustrating that still today so much of the expert medical communities, the people that can have a big impact on the community's health, still have the old mantra that nutrition has little impact on health and disease. It surprises me, as I don't know why they are so unwilling to let go and keep holding on to the old ways. I would suggest we ask the real experts on nutrition, the people who spent their whole life with animals, some of whom have for generations, these are the farmers. These are the people who really know animals and the impact of feed on their growth, health and vitality. I've been able to speak to many of them over the years and I would challenge you to do the same.

Ask any one of them, does the feed or grasses have any effect on the cow's milk or the taste of the beef? Does the feed have any effect on the hardness of a chickens egg? Does food quality have any effect on a dog or horse's coat? Of course it does! Yet, the human experts don't seem to think food has an impact on people's health. Baffling! Thus so many people continue to suffer and not be able to live up to their full potential and have a better quality of life. And this was the case with dogs as well until not to long ago.

I've seen it over and over with so many animals; simply changing the diet, adding more of the good oils and voilà, so many things would change. Their weight, their coat, their gums and teeth and often their neurotic behaviors would improve or dissipate. Dogs have a shorter life span than humans, thus they have an accelerated life. You can see the impact of nutrition faster in them. You can see the importance of nutrition on their health and how they age. Feed a dog table scraps and they get fat, develop teeth and gum problems, joint issues and chronic health issues such as heart disease and diabetes. Same thing happens in humans just at a slower pace so we don't seem to notice it. Have you heard the old riddle, how do you boil a frog? Slowly!

As my interests in different aspects of nutrition evolved a funny feeling came over me, why was I so obsessed with nutrition, biochemistry and now neurochemistry? The answer came one day when I was in my late forties after a conversation with my older brother. "Do you ever worry about going crazy like dad?" I asked him. "A little bit but not too much" he said. "I do. I think to myself, are my genes going to turn on some weird protein that turns me from Dr. Jekyll into Mr. Hyde? Am I going to start going crazy and attacking people around me? Will I end up living on the street?" With assuring words he reminded me that dad was sick. He had an illness and that we would be ok. I felt a bit better with his answer. Yet, I still had trepidations. and I still wondered if it was going to happen to me. I wanted to find out if some biochemical time bomb was going to shift my brain chemistry and make me crazy, and thus the personal interest for my own preservation lead to the interest in neurochemistry. It's hard to ignore strong emotional events that could potentially foreshadow one's own life path.

(*I use the word crazy here as I'm speaking from a youth's perspective, one without the understanding or knowledge of the variety and differences in mental health diseases and disorders.)

Maybe there is more to understand my drive. You see, being ten years old and seeing your father during a "crazy attack" or "breakdown" when he took take a knife and slit our mother's forehead open isn't the nicest thing. Seeing a man who had great skills, who had designed wonderful buildings, including many churches, who had multiple languages and talents loose it all and end up living on the streets of Toronto isn't that nice. Seeing the dominant male figure in your life turn into a non-productive, emotionless zombie isn't that inspiring either. It tore our family apart. And it was damn scary thinking I might turn out the same!

I now feel a real sadness for the man and those with these biochemical conditions that are expressed as mental illness. Yes I had a self interest in my own mental health, however, I now believe that what I had really wanted to figure out was what made his genes shift and created the negative impact in his brain chemistry and alter his behaviour. I wanted to help the man who I blamed for making my life so miserable which in turn altered my path in life which then made my life so fulfilling and rewarding. Funny, how the unconscious mind can drive our behaviour.

Twist Of Fate

No one could have predicted that such a simple challenge such as having a dog with a digestive intestinal issue would have contributed to me becoming so deeply interested in nutrition and nutritional biochemistry and how this would put me on such a different path in my life. I'm so thankful that this happened, as without this life lesson it is possible that I would have continued to suffer with chronic joint pain. I never would have seen or understood the deeper connections of food to health and I never would have explored the ways to optimize human potential with nutrition or how to address the underlying cause of diseases versus just treating the symptoms with medications. And who knows, without optimizing my nutrition I too may have ended up going "crazy" and living on the streets.

Remember when they used to tell us, "It doesn't matter what you eat. Food is just calories." As I've learned, food is so much more than just "calories". Food contains information in the form of phytonutrients, pigments, fats and other compounds that impact and "talk" to your genes modifying gene expression and how your body functions. This is called Nutrigenomics.

Think about this, certain fats you eat can promote inflammation in the body and others can reduce it. Food is one of the biggest determinants of your health and your dog's wellbeing. Low quality food, which is processed, refined, void of phytonutrients, fibers etc., has poor gene signaling information. It makes you and your dog inflamed. High quality food with lots of veggies, fruits, phytonutrients, good unprocessed fats, leaner proteins etc. has high quality gene signaling information. You express your genes in a more supporting way. Simply put, junk food contributes to poor or unhealthy gene expression with corresponding poor heath and chronic disease. High quality food contributes to optimized gene expression, better health, less chronic illness and a better quality of life. Every culture on the planet knows you are what you eat.

No one is more aware of this than devoted dog owners and the manufactures of dog foods. Simply look at the newer dogs foods; they are amazing compared to what was available even ten years ago. Loaded with inflammation reducing antioxidants, lots of good fats (omega 3 fish oils), joint support nutrients, less grains, better carbohydrate sources, and better protein sources. Heck, I would eat these newer foods over fast foods or in a pinch on a camping trip.

Would you believe that dogs could become allergic to food as well! Thus some of the newer foods have tailored protein sources for those animals with food allergies. Do you think humans could develop allergies to foods that would contribute to chronic health issues and that dietary changes could help them? We know this is true, yet some in the medical community still don't buy into this "theory". Baffling!

I recognize patterns and I can make simple observations. Over the last four decades I've worked and attended hundreds of seminars, tradeshows and conventions. And I've noticed something you might not believe. The pharmaccutical companies hire smart, talented and beautiful young people to represent their companies. (Smart marketing!) Interesting enough though, by far, the sickest, most run down and unhealthiest looking group of people I see are the physicians I see at these pharmaceutical trade shows. Why is this? Are they practicing what they preach? Food for thought and health isn't it!

If you've owned a dog you may have met these people. They're very special and unique indeed. They seem to care more about their dogs than themselves or other humans in their life. They will do anything for their dogs yet they let themselves slip downhill. Why do you think this is? I sure don't understand it. Maybe they just don't prioritize their own health and end up putting it on the back burner as they look after their dogs. Maybe they may not want to be perceived as "selfish". To put things into perspective, if you don't look after yourself you may end up rundown and burnt out. How will you help others then? If you don't want to be a burden on others because of sickness why not treat yourself better. Change the word *selfish to self-care*. The healthier you are, the more you can give and help others and your dog!

Do you feel worthy of self-care and love? Many don't feel this because of past experiences or negative conditioning. Because of my life events I know I struggled with this for many years. However, can I prove to you that you are worthy and loved? It's a simple experiment. Call your dog over and give them a pat. Say their name and see what they do. What does your dog think of you? They think you're an amazing dog owner and caregiver! Probably the best ball thrower and walker ever! And you are. Just the fact that you're reading a book like this proves you care and are a compassionate person who is worthy and loved. It's a give and take relationship. You're a great caregiver and a great care-receiver.

Dogs give us unconditional love and companionship, they get us out into nature, they get us socializing with other dog walkers and in return we want to keep them around as long as possible. We want to keep them healthy so we "invest" in their health with good high quality foods and walks. Why not invest in our own health and do this for ourselves?

Working in a busy animal hospital that had 20, 30, 40 or more animals come through the doors everyday for years exposes you to a large sample size of animal issues. You get to see many different illnesses and diseases. Patterns emerge that we can learn from. A common pattern I saw in aging dogs revolved around the owner's beliefs on aging. If they thought aging and getting old was about watching TV, taking it easy, not doing too much, enjoying the fruits of life, and treating themselves to treats and snacks then their animals lived the same way and thus they didn't fare as well. These dogs had way more issues with diabetes, kidney disease, cardiovascular issues and cancer. As I've gone through life this exact same pattern happens in humans. Depending on your point of view, do we get the same disease as the dogs or do they get the same disease as us! Interesting question isn't it?

As a side note, have you ever been over at a friend's home, or maybe in your own home, and as dinner or the BBQ progresses the dogs starts circling around waiting for their share of the goods? You can hear the knife clink on the plate as the owner starts scraping the table scraps onto one plate or into the dog's bowl. The dog is drooling at this point anticipating the feast its about to gorge on when out of left field someone yells, "Don't feed the dogs scraps. It'll make them sick". That's right; don't feed the dog that crappy human food it will make them sick, but it's ok for us to eat it everyday for years. More food for thought!

Another observation that surprises me is that we can call a dog fat and put it on a diet to better its health, yet we don't do this with ourselves. Many are afraid of the "F" word (fat). If we care about someone and call them out on a bad habit or health condition aren't we being a good friend? We aren't teasing or putting them down, we care about them and we want to help them right? If I asked you the question, "Do you know three things you could do to improve your health?" most would quickly name them. Yet interesting enough, many don't apply the information in our day-to-day living in ourselves. Why not? What's holding us back? To know something is valuable and important to do and yet, to not do it, is to not know its value.

If you haven't yet, is now the time to invest in better food for your dog, your loyal pet who is your best friend and buddy, the one who loves you and knows you're worthy? Is now the time to invest a little TLC (tender loving care) in yourself with better food for your health? You know it makes a difference in dogs and you know it will make a difference in you, so why not invest in your health today?

Maybe we all need to start being a little kinder to ourselves. Would it hurt if we all stop being so hard on ourselves and gave ourselves some credit for all the hard work we do. Is now the time for a little self-care for you? After all, we're pretty good dog owners aren't we! You could start with something small or go all out and make major changes. Your choice! Treat yourself right, you deserve it.

The body and mind are connected. Moving the body can increase blood flow, boost endorphins and other brain hormones that improve our mood so we feel better. Motion generates emotion. If you don't like how you are feeling… move differently. Dance, exercise, air guitar sing or whatever and you will feel better! I would suggest taking the dog for a walk or run!

Feed your mind good stuff at the end of each day to boost your sense of wellbeing and gratitude. Call your dog over and simply think about how lucky we are to have these amazing dogs in our lives and how they wonderfully enrich our lives. Where would we be without them? As well, think about how lucky they are to have us as their awesome owners! This is a beautiful win-win situation! Isn't this great food for thought? What a good attitude and mindset to have.

LESSON 3
Attitude and Mindset

I noticed it in the distance. Its twitchy movement caught my eye so I slowly knelt down beside Max and slowly pointed in the direction where it was. He made visual contact and started to shake. His body went tense as his muscles readied to explode. He knew what was going to unfold. Ever so slowly I slid my hand down the leather leash to his collar and carefully reached over and undid the brass clip connected to his collar. His shaking was now amplified. I too was getting excited; this was going to be good. I held his collar with one hand, as he was already trying to lurch and surge forward. I whispered steady. Steady! A million years of evolution and deep primal instincts were about to unfold in his body perfectly designed for running and hunting. In one quick motion I released him and yelled… SQUIRREL!

Each time it unfolded almost the same. Each time he put his heart and soul into the task, and each time he "failed", he never got the squirrel. But that never stopped him or any other dog I've had from giving it their best. Trying their hardest and putting forth their best effort seems to be in their nature. Even when my first dog Lady was 15 years old, stiff with arthritis and pain, when we went to the park and she saw a squirrel the chase was on. She pushed through the pain, discomfort and put her heart and soul into that ten-second chase.

I loved the enthusiasm, focus and attitude that Max and other dogs adopt in daily tasks or events. It really is something to be admired and learned from. Don't believe me? Say to any dog, in any language in any part of the world… "Want to go for a walk?" or even simpler, just say one word "WALK". Watch for the reaction. I think we can all agree that a dog's happy and sunny attitude towards mundane tasks can be a benchmark and model for us to learn from. What would happen it we reacted this way when someone yelled… WORK!

A famous quote by Vince Lombardi goes… "If you aren't fired with enthusiasm then you will be *fired* with enthusiasm!" This dovetails nicely with another quote "Nothing great was ever achieved without enthusiasm" by Ralph Waldo Emerson. Yes, dogs taught me how important mindset and attitude are at improving the quality of our life in so many different areas.

Max had been with us for just a few years. It was 2013 and the mirror reminded me I was older and now 53. Max was our first family dog that we chose with our kids. He was part mini poodle and part Golden-doodle. He had a wonderful wavy golden coat and long white hair that flowed in the wind from this tail as he ran. Max had been with us a few years. I affectionately called him the "son" I never had. He was a perfect first dog for the kids, kind, very gentle, patient, good natured and happy. He was great to have around with his sunny and uplifting attitude. He was always up for a walk, weather be dammed. His happy nature and good vibrations radiated into all that were around him, including me. Nothing seemed to get him down. His attitude was such a joy to experience and having him around was a blessing for all in his presence. He was special all right.

I remember so clearly sitting down after a very frustrating week at work. There had been poor weather conditions, business had been really slow, many cancelled their appointments and now my boss was on my case and wanted a few reports on Monday, which meant my weekend was going to be shot as I had to do a few "stupid" reports. I felt resentful. To drive home the stake of discontentment, I muttered under my breath "I hate this job" but I needed the money so I had to stay. My attitude sucked. To clear my negative thoughts and reboot my mood I decided to have a good walk with Max. This I knew would change my attitude, as I didn't want to be *fired* with enthusiasm! I needed a new attitude and mindset. I needed to look at the world a new way. My dogs were a good source of positive mindset. I wondered how I could be like Max and have a better outlook and attitude towards work and life in general.

On the walk is when I started asking some new questions about my work and things changed with my attitude. I started reflecting on the time my older brother once humbled me and stated I was lucky to have a job and that many would gladly take it if I didn't want it. Toronto was a big fast growing city and there were lots of keen people who would gladly step up into my job. I started thinking that maybe I was lucky to have a job as so many didn't. Hmmm, since I have to go to work everyday I wonder how I could make my work more enjoyable and even fun! I decided I was going to have more fun and fulfillment everyday when I went to work. Right then and there I changed my mindset from "I have to go to work" to that of "I get to go play, socialize, have fun, contribute and enjoy my day as I get paid for it!" This simple mindset change in me was a HUGE game changer. I started to happily achieve! Max was a great role model for this. It seemed I had to relearn this lesson many times in my life.

I got out a piece of paper and started writing down all the people and accounts that I wanted to work with and those that I didn't. I made a list of the things I had control of and could change in my daily tasks. I brainstormed all the ways I could boost my enjoyment and happiness as I went about my day. How could I use my car as a mobile classroom and fill my brain with proactive positive thoughts and stories? I wrote down the subjects and areas I wanted to learn about and went about getting tapes on them. (Thank goodness for audio books on tapes, CD's and now podcasts.) I decided on the tasks that I had to let go and stop doing that made me frustrated. Some of the other things I didn't like doing I did my best to delegate or even pay others to do them for me. I also decided to really focus on separating my work and home life worlds. I wouldn't play at work and I wouldn't work at play (home life). This was super critical for my sanity and peace of mind.

My life experiences with dogs taught me that you could turn everyday, mundane tasks into moments of great pleasure and satisfaction if you put your heart into it and if you have the right attitude. As I've travelled through life, this lesson would go on to serve me very well. Alas though, as a sad observation, many seem to have missed this lesson which is so important for our happiness. Living in Ghetto Village in my early twenties with my dogs Lady and Casy I got "schooled" in this fundamental lesson of life. I would have to learn it many times.

Attitude Is Key To Almost Everything

Like a sharp pointy stone in your shoe it kept bothering me and never went away. I would dwell on this idea for extended periods of time. It generated a lot of bitterness, resentment and frustration in me. Actually, I would even say anger. I just couldn't let it go. When I went out, everything reminded me of it. Every time I was hanging out with friends at one of their homes it surfaced. I just couldn't understand it.

I kept asking myself, was I being punished for some reason? Was I a bad person? Was I not worthy of good things in my life? How come I had so many problems? How come I was poor? How come life wasn't fair to me? Ah, that was the problem. It was my attitude. I thought life was supposed to be fair. Not so. Life indeed wasn't fair. I deeply wanted it to be, but because it wasn't I was pissed and angry right back at it. A crappy attitude was filling my brain leading to a poor mindset, erroneous thinking and detrimental behaviour.

Some might call it maturity, growing up or even evolving. I called it giving in. I was in a rut; beat down and I simply gave in. I was starting to wallow in self-pity. I kept thinking (whining) "poor me." It was hard accepting the fact that life isn't fair and that's just the way things are. Accepting this fact and facing the truth was tough for me. It was another jagged bitter pill to swallow. As I was learning, those that need help aren't always the ones that get help.

Remembering back to the late 60's and early 70's pot was easy to come by. It seemed like it was everywhere and the attitude from the aging hippies was it was cool and liberating to use. It was groovy. Some smoked cigarettes, I choose pot. And of course we drank the booze we stole from our parents. These were great escape agents from my home life.

It had been almost a decade now. Pot, booze, psychedelics and other chemicals were an almost daily past time. They were the essence of my world and it was shrinking down on me. I was suffocating. I was becoming more frustrated and angry with my life. I didn't know how to deal with much of society. I was lashing out at people. I hated where I was at. My attitude sucked. I wanted out.

We can all handle one or maybe two issues but I was overwhelmed. A broken heart from a lost first love, a deep debilitating depression fueled by alcohol and drugs, a raunchy and depressing living environment, no work, a life time of people telling you you're no good, worthless and so on, a dog I didn't want and now the negative mindset of a future with no hope or potential weighted heavily on my shoulders like a ton of bricks. It was crushing me. There was nothing left in inside to push back with. The tank was empty. I was more desperate than ever to get out. The hardware store had the tools I needed.

The garage was damp, cold and dark just like my attitude towards the world. I was going to the woods to make my exit. I had gathered up the things I was going to need; rope, stool, knife, paper and…. Where's the frigging pen? Hesitantly I crept back inside to get a pen. As I was slinking out of the house with the pen that damn puppy came out of nowhere greeting me with her big brown eyes, perked up ears and tail wagging with that look; Walk? "Not now" I scolded. "Get out of the way". Lady was normally very sensitive and timid but this evening she stood her ground and continued to "ask" to be taken out. Dogs just have that look when they have to go. I could feel the tug of responsibility nudging me along. I grumbled under my breath and blurted, "Alright let's go". We left and walked towards the woods.

I'm not sure what happened on that walk down by the river that night but I had time to re-evaluate what I was about to do. Was it worth it? Did I have the guts to pull it off? I was pretty sure the world wouldn't miss me but what would my brothers and mom think and who would look after the dog? Damn it's my dog now. I'm supposed to look after her. Crap. I didn't want this frigging dog. Puppies are so cute and adorable we all fall in love with them and I was no different. Lady was undeniably cute and loveable. The powerful desire to nurture new life overpowered my desperate thoughts to end life.

I was deeply stirred down to my core with all that was going through my mind. This dog had sent an arrow into my heart and now I felt indebted to her for changing the course of my life. I didn't know it at the time but my attitude was being shifted. "Lady Luck" had done her thing. She changed the course of my life and gave me a new perspective towards my beliefs and attitude. I often reflect on how lucky I was to have this dog come into my life at this key moment. Just after my walk in the woods with Lady, when I hit my rock bottom I was deeply moved and realized that things had to change.

It might have been the purple psychedelic pills that gave me this insight but I can remember thinking in one of my anger rages, "F-THIS! LIFE SUCKS!" I don't want to put up with this shit anymore. I'm going to dig myself out of this pile of crap. I'm going to push back and say F-U to everyone and the world. If this is the game, if this is how it is, then I'll play by new rules. I hit a threshold that caused a shift in my mindset and attitude. I got me a whole new philosophy! I had to clean up my act and get my shit together.

I stopped boozing and polluting my body with drugs and this had very different consequences than what I would have expected. It revealed who my actual friends were. My whole identify for the last decade had been caught up in my partying activities. Now I still went to parties, I still was hanging out with my "friends" but the dynamics were changing.

The fall evening air was crisp and cool. The leaves were already falling and it got dark earlier so we could start the party sooner. It was one of those typical Saturday nights. Darcy's parents were away at the cottage so twenty or so of us descended upon his house. But something was different now. There was a huge pressure to have just one drink, one joint, one hit. "Come on Robbie, join the fun". "What's with you man?" All of a sudden there was a weird vibe in the group. I wasn't partaking so I wasn't fitting in; I wasn't one of them anymore. The common denominator was broken. Then the teasing started and it was followed by harassments and even fights. Defending this new boundary was extremely difficult. I was growing, changing and morphing into someone new. They didn't seem to like my new attitude and the new me and funny enough, I didn't seem to like them either. Just like how a snake can only keep growing if it sheds it's limiting skin, I to needed to shed my old skin of friends to keep growing.

Growing up can be tough. Just like a good swift kick in the pants, the light bulb went off as it hit me, life isn't fair! Life isn't just. Life isn't easy. Too bad for me, just suck it up and get used to it. My attitude was being turned upside down and backwards. This reality check was another tough jagged pill to swallow. It hurt going down and it churned my viscera inside out. I didn't want to accept it or live it. I wasn't used to taking responsibility for my situation or my actions. This caused me a lot of stomach aches but funny enough, and this was the perplexing part, it gave me an inner peace and solitude that I had never experienced before. I became much calmer with a new inner strength. I had to accept the raw fact that life isn't fair or easy. As tough as it was, I was adopting a new attitude.

And once I accepted this fact, a funny thing happened, and it's hard to believe, but life got easier! It's hard to explain but this mindset of acceptance made it easier to go about my day. I just adopted the attitude that everything is going to be tough for me so get used to it. I would just have to put up with more crap and work harder than others to get ahead. Like the dogs, I would just go about my day and not let things bother me so much. I was learning to go with the flow. I begrudgingly accepted the fact that life is tough and instead of asking for it to be easier, I started working on building myself up to be a stronger person with more skills so I could handle the bumps and challenges easier. I had to get bigger than my problems.

Working with the dogs and seeing their enthusiasm towards our training time and understanding that from their perspective, they weren't being "trained". They were just playing and having fun with us. It was their attitude towards the whole process that made the difference. This observation is something I was starting to adopt. And this was making a significant impact in how my days unfolded and the quality of my life.

Little did I know that this life lesson of positive attitude and outlook that I picked up from my dogs would carry me though many, many storms. It helped build up in me a mental toughness. It gave me grit and determination that came through in my persistence to achieve my goals in life. It allowed me to carry on when I didn't think I could. It helped build discipline into my psyche. Like a psychedelic drug trip the insights I was getting were profound.

It was a strange "aha" moment when I noticed that my thoughts led to certain feelings that led to corresponding actions and results. My negative thoughts often led to negative results. However, when I really focused my thoughts on the positives, on the end goal or dream, and really generated the warm and fuzzy feelings surrounding obtaining them, my actions and intent generated positive results. As strange and corny as it might sound, I was learning how to turn my dreams into reality.

With the right focus and mindset I could make the little things I wanted materialize and happen! How cool is that! These were mostly just small tiny wins of no real significance but they put me on the right path. And the feelings of empowerment were incredible. Slow as it was, I was getting control of my attitude and my life. And the key to all this was, I was starting to generate some momentum. Many small tiny wins were adding up and fueling me on. It was easier to keep the ball rolling. My outlook and mindset were slowly shifting and the more time I spent with the dogs the better it was getting.

In hindsight, I'm so grateful that my life started out the way that it did for me. I often think, "How lucky am I that all this "negative" stuff happened to me early on?" It exposed me to the tough "reality check" lessons of life and it gave me time to apply and refine my skills at using them. It built my coping skills, helped me develop internal resources and the fortitude to deal with life events. In a sense, I learned how to deal with all the crap, got it out of my system, learned from it and then I moved on. How lucky was I!

The fall of 1980 was the first year of me working at the animal hospital. It was awkward. I felt very troubled with some of the pressures I was experiencing. Despite my resistance towards their suggestion, the Vets at the animal hospital continued to encourage me to go back to school. They could see something in me that I couldn't see in myself. My attitude and beliefs told me I couldn't do it. I wasn't smart enough, I would get laughed at and be a fool for trying, it would be hard, how could I afford to not work and go to school? It was too big of a problem for me to handle. I still had a lot of self-doubt and felt unworthy of such a task.

One of the younger vets, Dr. Mark Cole, was persistent and continued to nudge me forward. I succumbed to the pressures and thank goodness I took their good advice. Considering I thought I knew it all, I didn't know how much I didn't know and how important this event was going to be in my life. Going back to grade ten high school when you're twenty with the goal of become a Vet requires a positive mindset, blind faith, a new attitude and a big why! Returning to school in the winter semester of 1981 was my new goal. It was going to be the start of a new chapter in my life. Now all I had to do was apply.

Your Why

I couldn't help but focus on her eyes; the glasses made them huge. They were a bright emerald green and piercing. You don't see them too often so they stuck in my mind. She was looking at me though these glasses that looked like something from a Far Side cartoon. You know the ones, "cat" like, turning up to points at the sides and they stuck out past the sides of her head, with thick black rims. Her hair is what I remember the most though. It was blonde and very straight all the way down to her shoulders. It would have draped over them and her back if she hadn't curled it out to the sides in perfect little upward curls that bounded as she spoke. Very "Far Side-ish". If you were a flea her hair would have made an amazing slide. This was the high school guidance counselor who could help shape my life and help me make my dream come true. She was to be my trusted advisor!

She leaned forward towards me as to make sure I heard her and to make sure others didn't. In a softer voice than she had been using, she quietly shared, "I wanted to be a Vet. It's a tough program to get into. I spent years trying. Welding is a good career so why don't you just go up to the college and get your welding papers!" I was 20 years old applying to grade 10 and this guidance counselor was looking at my school history, my job record and at me, and not seeing much of a future. She didn't see me becoming a vet. What she saw was me going to welding school to become a welder.

I couldn't help think about her lack of will power and motivation. She must have given it the old college try and failed and now seeing me, a guy who was in a worse state than I'm sure she had been, assumed that there was no way in hell I could made it. She broke the news to me gently. "Go get your welding papers". Incredible! Not something positive and supporting like "Hey young man this is going to be a tough go, you're going to need some serious motivation, resources and mentors. I'll help get you on the right path." No, none of that. It was at that moment I thought "Ha! It sucks to be you!" She didn't have the internal drive. She didn't have a big enough why. She had the wrong attitude.

I had this powerful thought; I can't let this person's limiting beliefs limit me. She failed at her attempt and because she didn't see the potential in me based on my dress code and history she thought I would fail as well. She never asked about my "why", my motivation or my vision.

There was so much to learn and so much I didn't know, it really was overwhelming, but I wasn't going to let it stop me from doing the few things I could do. I would out work and out study the others to make up for my slow learning and limited skills. I would have to work twice as hard, but I had a bigger why. I had a clear vision of where I wanted to now go and was feeling uplifted because of my new mindset and attitude. I knew the path. They say the toughest part of any journey is the first step. So I made the tough decision. I took the first step along the path and enrolled into grade 10 high school at age twenty. My journey was beginning.

How We Label Ourselves

What level of your potential do you feel you're you living up to? 100%? 60%? 30%? Do you think you could bump it up a notch, say just 10%? How many wonderful ways would this change your life for the better? I surface this because I was living way below my potential but I didn't know it at the time. My beliefs and attitude limited my vision of myself. They "clouded" my perspectives and tainted my ability to see a positive future. At this point in my life my vision of my future was bleak. The beliefs I had of my abilities, and my worthiness were nil. Confidence levels were at zero. I felt I had no potential.

Now here is the key lesson that changed so much for me and I hope it empowers and serves you well. What I never realized is that my self-definition, the way I described myself, wasn't my definition! The beliefs I had about myself weren't mine. The beliefs I had were the labels and names others had given and put on me (loser, bum, slow learner, trouble, druggie, Ghetto child etc.). As I discovered, you must understand this vital concept of beliefs, attitude and mindset if you want to be happy and fulfilled in your life.

Why is this so important? We grow into the labels we and others give ourselves. We live into our beliefs about what we can and can't do! They impact what we will and won't do- the actions we do or don't take. These beliefs moderate what level of potential we live up to. Bottom line, the beliefs and labels we have of ourselves are everything.

The old saying that sticks and stones can break your bones but words can never hurt is blatantly wrong. I could recover from a physical injury but the deep damage of the words (labels) was killing me. These words and labels others had placed on me had crumbled my self-esteem leaving me feeling defeated and unworthy of anything positive. Their biting sting was venom to my soul. I was living into the ways they described me. The poor social environment I was in was programing me.

You can try and deny this influence but its insidious nature penetrates your fragile spirit. I bought into and started believing these poisonous words. This wasn't who I was at my core but their labels became my beliefs and lead to my non-supporting actions! And that severely limited my future and my potential. And here is the kicker, something you must understand; I didn't know this was happening, it was all sub-conscious. I was running on someone else's autopilot program. This had to change for me to move forward. I had to deal with my inner voice.

Gremlins - Our Self Talk

Going back to school made me very uncomfortable. There were kids four years younger in my classes, including my youngest brother Peter and some of his friends. I felt I was the big dummy in the crowd and they all knew it. My gremlins were making havoc in my mind. There is a powerful quote from about three hundred years ago by John Milton that puts this into perspective; "The mind is its own place and in itself can make a heaven of hell or a hell of heaven." Apparently we all have it, those little inner voices that talk to us, our "conscious" if you will, just sitting there on our shoulder, always talking. And often they seem to keep focusing on doubt and fear. This limits our ability to believe in our own skills and talents so we stop taking "risks" and trying. I didn't want to hear the gremlins anymore but they kept shouting! I had to acknowledge them and then I did my best to ignore them. As I got better at this, I replaced and reprogramed them with my own cheerleading squad that reinforced the faith and beliefs that I had in me! Almost by accident I discovered a few things that became my go to supports.

The new way I discovered how to lift my spirits and boost my confidence was by falling back to the few simple things I seemed to be good at and that made me feel good. The things I was confident about; training the dogs, running and riding motorcycles. Whenever I felt crappy or down or if the gremlins were winning the battle with my attitude, I would go work with the dogs, go riding or both! Seems I had to do this a lot. My battered ego and limiting "injured" beliefs needed some serious help. This was the spark to a bigger dream for my future.

As I was lucky enough to discover, when you have self-doubt or feel like you are lacking confidence, go back to what you are good at. Do this to build your confidence and shift your attitude into a positive state. Then go back and attack your challenge with new eyes and a new mindset of confidence; "I got this". If can do that other thing well then I can do this new thing just as well!

We are born into an environment that we have no control over. The circumstances set the stage of how we are shaped. However, the good news is our mindset, attitude and philosophies are pliable. We can obtain full control of our life by applying our will to shape, build and construct the environment that we want. We can take back control of the circumstances that shapes our life. We can look into the future to plan and make happen the environment that will shape us in the ways we desire. If we don't like our present situation, we can close this chapter of our life and write a new chapter on a blank page. We can write the story of the supporting future we want and then live into it! How cool is that! And please remember, it all starts with choosing to do it. The confidence I was developing from working with the dogs was paying off. My attitude was changing; I was building up my mental strength to push back and to silence the gremlins and redefine who I was.

The power of our self-talk is life altering. Just like how a song can get stuck in your head. It just keeps playing over and over again and you can't get rid of it. I had to get control and squash the negative sound tract that was playing in my head. It needed to be short circuited and reprogramed. But how do you reprogram the beliefs running around in your head? I didn't know how, but what I did know is this, I wasn't going to let my past be my future. My attitude and mindset were becoming more supportive. I was going to change somehow and redefine myself. I had to take back control and redefine myself, my way, in a more positive and supporting way. It was empowering to now understand that the beliefs we have of ourselves are not fixed! They can morph and develop as we grown and change through our life, if we chose to change them. This was vital for me at the tender age of twenty to finally "get it". I got it, a new mindset.

Modern psychology has shared that we will never rise above the image and vision we have of our future and ourselves. This applies in any area of our life. You will live up to but not beyond your vision. How we see ourselves is what we become. Children will only be as grand as the vision we have for them. Without a positive vision your potential for a positive future will perish. That's where I was at and thank goodness that the vets saw something in me and planted the seeds of a better future. They helped shape my vision of what was possible for me. It's up to you to help our children (and inner children) build and imagine positive uplifting futures for them. Our visions and dreams are important to pull us forward through both the good and bad times.

Vision

How does a building get built? Someone has to first imagine it finished. They have to be able to see it completed in their mind. They have to "see" it before it's a reality. Then they can draw detailed plans on how to go about building it. Finally they start the building process. There is an understanding that there will be hiccups along the way. They simply modify their plan, readjust and carry on until the project is finished. I believe that life is the same way. You have to have a vision of how you want your life to be, and then you draw out a plan to build your life. Finally you go about making it happen. Stuff or hiccups will happen. Not a big deal. You reevaluate and modify your plan a bit and carry on. Challenges aren't stop signs, they're re-evaluation points. Finally, just like that, your vision is turned into reality. As I found out, if you aren't living your true vision, you will be building and living someone else's plan.

Regaining control of my beliefs and how I saw myself was vital for my progression. There was so much I couldn't control yet there were a few things I could. So that's where I focused my energy. I also started to realize I had more control of my life than I thought. I wasn't going to let the things I couldn't do stop me from doing the things I could. I had to eat so I was going to start eating the best foods I could. Working out made me feel good so I would do that. If I couldn't ride the dirt bikes, I would run or build myself up by lifting weights. I could go to the library and read the books I wanted on the information I wanted to learn. And, I would spend time training the dogs as they gave me so much joy and love that my starving soul desperately needed. Thank god (that's dog spelt backwards) for dogs and their unconditional love. I desperately had to find the good in me and they helped me do it. Their attitude and mindset towards life was rubbing off on me.

Changing the beliefs I had about myself was tough. The pain and hurt was debilitating. I wanted to escape and make the thoughts I had go away. I was always keeping myself busy with idle things to prevent myself from actually listening to what my inner voice was screaming to tell me. I had medicated myself to the point of being numb to avoid looking inward and listing to the inner voice.

You know that little voice we all hear in our heads? Mine is really chatty. Before it would use the negative words others used to describe me. But now, as I was working out it would find new words to describe me. When I ran it might say "speedy". On the dirt bikes it might say "smooth" or "flow". My spirit was starving, and weak. I was scrounging for every little morsel of confidence and positive that I could find to feed it. My self-talk became more encouraging and generous in how it described me. The phrases were all better than what it was saying before so I accepted them. I did the few things that I knew would give me positive feedback and were supporting to my soul. With this simple strategy I stopped doing the things that caused negative self-talk or a negative self-image and reshaped my mindset.

No one told me and as strange as it seemed, I never knew I could change my life path. I thought the story of my life had been written for me and was carved in stone. Things were the way they were. That was just how life was. Some call it destiny. In hindsight I don't understand why they didn't tell me. Or, maybe they did and I just didn't get it or maybe I didn't listen to them. They never empowered me with this key life principle. Not my parents, the teachers at the school, the counselors, the police. No one told me that I could actually exert my own free will to guide my future, that I actually had a choice. I could choose!

You could go for years of child therapy and childhood regression analysis or you can just decide and choose a better more supporting life. It's that simple. I did and you can too. Just start questioning every belief you have. Reprogram your inner voice so it's more supporting and shed your old skin to make way for the new. Do the things that make your soul sing. Feed your body and mind positives. If you don't like something about your life, you can close this chapter and write a new story of how you want your life to be. It's a blank slate. You can do and be anything you want. But you have to choose and you have to take action. You have to get fired with enthusiasm! How lucky are you that you now know one secret to a happier life! Just like with my dogs, attitude was key to happiness.

For me, I discovered that salvation was in leveraging the future. Thinking about what positive things could be in my life. Seeing how others lived and acted and then using that as a role model, dreaming about what could potentially be for me was the carrot. I had to have this inspiring vision. But this wasn't enough. I couldn't reach the carrot. I might have set the bar too high, as my deflated ego kept saying, "No way! You'll never get there or have that. Give up and stop wasting your time. Loser." The experts say we are more than two times likely to move away from pain (the stick) than we are to move towards pleasure (the carrot). The carrot wasn't enough for me. I needed a bigger push, a bigger motivation. I needed a bigger stick (pain). And I knew a place I could get one, my past. I decided to use all the negatives in my past as fuel for my launch. I was going to get me one big ass stick.

My past was driving me. I was running from it, yet I could never get away. I couldn't hide it or hide from it. It was always there nipping at my heels driving my behaviour in ways I didn't always like. To accept who I am, to learn how to love myself and to be happy in my own skin I needed to take action and face the truth and get rid of this skeleton.

It was time to step up. I realized I could never be free to make my own future until I stopped blaming others for my problems and situation. I realized I couldn't blame, complain or justify my situation or results anymore. I had to step up and take full responsibility for everything in my life, the good, the bad and the ugly. I had to squash the doubt and negative soundtrack that was running through my head. I had to find the good in myself. Changing is tough but a better attitude helped move me forward.

This was easy to say but very hard to do. I didn't have healthy role models. I didn't know how to act right thus it seemed I needed a new script or a new playbook on how to act in more proactive and socially appropriate ways! I tried my ways but they weren't working. I needed some new ways of being.

If I wanted more in life I would have to hunker down, and do whatever it takes. The sacrifices, the hard work, whatever it took I was going to do it. I would have to take full control of all areas of my life. If I wanted respect I was going to have to earn it with hard work. I was going to become response-able!

To get to the point of being free of my past and the hold it had on me I felt I had to turn and face it. I couldn't run from it anymore. I couldn't hide from it. It was a poison inside that was killing me. I decided I had to run to this fear and face it. I had to turn to it for power. I wanted to turn my struggles into strengths. I had to engulf it, digest it and use it for internal power. I needed to somehow learn how to turn my troubles into treasure and use them as a source of strength, insight and motivation. And yes, even humor! I believed this would set me free to live my life on my terms without all the weight of baggage. It allowed me to set my own willful direction in my life to regain control of a sinking ship. What a relief! What an attitude! Working with my dogs helped me see and understand this core concept.

I would suggest to you that if you want to get control of your life and be the captain of your own ship, run to your fears and tackle them as they unconsciously control your behaviour and the direction of your life. Otherwise you don't really have control; you're just the passenger. These fears limit your choices. In life you get what you settle for. Don't settle for less than your dreams. Build yourself a new more supporting attitude.

I was labeled a slow learner; I had a serious addiction with drugs and alcohol and to boot, I was deep in trouble with the law because of a crappy attitude and the plain stupid things I did. I had no skills, no money and was at the bottom of a deep rut close to the edge. There was really no chance of me pulling out of it. Most thought my potential was zero. At that point, I had nothing and was nothing. Yet now, I'm sharing and teaching doctors about advanced therapeutic nutrition, and nutrigenomics. I teach workshops on cancer prevention, I was able to obtain high levels in 2 different sports, I've become good at sculpting and photography, I'm still fit and lean, I don't need to take any medications for high blood pressure or cholesterol, I've been married to my wife of 23+ years (someone actually fell for me!), and our kids are turning out ok. We have a deep sense of fulfillment and satisfaction with our life. We feel good as we have peace of mind and contentment with the life we've made. And that's the key point; the life we've *chosen* to make! Attitude makes all the difference in ones life. This is one thing I learned from all the dogs in my life.

I don't say this to impress you, rather I say it to impress upon you, to drive home the point, anything can happen if you want to make it happen, if you have a big enough why. You don't have to know how it's going to happen. You don't have to know all the steps to get there, but you do have to decide to take action however small each day and move forward. You must keep moving forward into the unknown. You need a vision of how you want the future to unfold for you. You need a why!

How is it that water can erode rock? It seems impossible yet it happens everyday, all the time and has from day one on the planet. How does this happen? Small, simple insignificant things done day in day out, over and over compounding over the long haul that's how. And I think it's the same in life. I'm not a rocket scientist, or the sharpest tool in the toolbox, but I'm getting good at seeing patterns. Time gives you experience and reflection. My experience with dogs has taught me this one key life lesson.

I've found that with small simple daily tasks, the boring and mundane, the unsexy and dull things, consistently repeated and applied over weeks, months and years translate into incredible changes. It was the purposeful and deliberate practice with a vision of where I wanted to go that built the grit and fortitude for me to carry on and work my way out of the rut my life was in.

There was always so much to do; I over estimated what I wanted to get done each day. It was hugely frustrating as I felt I was never getting everything done. I didn't feel like I was making any progress. However, and here is another key takeaway point that I learned, I grossly underestimated what could be done over years and decades. It is so amazing what we can achieve. I didn't understand how skills build upon each other and can accelerate your progress. Please, learn from my mistake! My attitude was so bad that I wasn't open to letting others help me. I wasted so much time struggling and trying to figure things out for myself. I don't want to think about how much time and how much farther ahead I would have been if I had just opened up to feedback, coaching and mentoring or others helping me. I'm sure I could have saved years if not a decade! I wasted so much time because of a bad attitude.

But now I know. As my age inches up to sixty, I realize I'm just getting started. I'm so jazzed and excited about what I'm going to make happen. I just can't wait to see what the next twenty years bring. And you can do this to. You just have to keep going. You have to stay hungry! A friend's mother has recently turned 80. She still goes to spinning and kickboxing classes and hangs out with forty year olds! Since her retirement at age sixty-five she has written something like 25 books! You go girl!

The Attitude Of Zen

In those tremulous years of my early twenties accepting that life is hard was a blessing. It completely shifted my attitude. I somehow found joy in the simple things that I did everyday. Walking the dogs, cleaning up after them, feeding them and so on. They had to be done so there was no point complaining about them, I just did them and moved on. After a while I got curious about how I could do them better or more efficiently or even make them fun. What else could I learn, how hard could I push my body, how long could I keep working without sleep and so on.

I've only just recently discovered that this is part of the Zen philosophy. There is even a quote "Before enlightenment, chop wood, carry water. After enlightenment, chop wood, carry water." For me this quote can be chunked down to "Find joy in the basic tasks you have to do everyday to get you to your goal or you will be miserable and bitter. And once you hit your goal, keep doing the basics to keep moving forward."

It seems everyone wants to start at the top, but let me ask you, if you can't handle the basic small stuff, how are you going to handle the big important things? Stuff has to be done so learn how to enjoy the task. Be present in the moment and enjoy the experience. Having and working with dogs kept this front of my mind. Their positive and uplifting attitude to the day is wonderful to be around. Finding joy in the simple daily tasks is key.

In reflection I can now see that many didn't have the opportunity to learn these lessons at an earlier age and apply them to their life. So now when they have financial issues, relationship problems, work problems or if they still haven't controlled their drinking, it crushes them. They don't have the internal skills or resources to overcome the challenge and the results are much more severe as we get older. They crash and can't get back up their feet.

Learning this idea from the dogs about attitude and mindset towards the day and life was so much more powerful that I understood or knew at the time. I can now say that I understand the idea of honoring the struggle; it will make you stronger and wiser. Expect that there will be hardship and decide that you will meet it as an opportunity to grow and show the world what you've got. Honor the big steps outside your comfort zone because they will make you better. Shifting my mindset from I'm scared to I'm excited for the new experiences and growth was not easy for me. I had to start very slowly and with very small steps. However, once I accepted that life is hard, life became easier.

Another interesting twist occurred when I took back some control of my life. Instead of hardships or struggles being imposed on me I did my best to take back control and apply them myself. I purposefully shaped the way I was growing and what skills I was going to learn and develop. You can to. I started setting new goals for myself (these were actually just tiny little steps forward). How much lactic acid burning can I handle in my legs when cycling? How many reps can I do with these weights? What interesting book do I want to read next? How many ways can I contribute and help animals? These were simple things I had control over and exerted my will to choose.

I didn't come up with a plan leading to some big goal. I came up with a "plan" to simply get started on these small simple little things. I knew I would have to make adjustments and reevaluations along the way. That's just the way it is.

Learning how to tolerate discomfort helped increase my confidence. My inner voice would say, "If I can handle this, then I can handle anything". Getting over complacency and being comfortable was very difficult to do. Doing things I didn't like, was afraid of or wasn't in the mood to do, or if my mindset said I was too tired, or it was going to be hard, was very hard to control. But I was desperate and I had a new why.

Your Choice

We all have a choice each morning. We can choose to stick to our normal routine, follow cravings, distractions and let our emotions dictate whether we workout, stick to our diet, or abandon our goals. Or we can choose to be better than yesterday even when it's uncomfortable or even painful. This is all I did. I took the all-important and vital first step, then another. Your mind will begin to strengthen and see the difference choices as opportunity for growth.

As I have found, your mind can be your biggest asset or your biggest weakness, your biggest stumbling block or hurdle to success if you don't take control and train it well. If you don't control your thoughts, the negative ones will run the show and lead you into a self-fulfilling prophecy of a negative situation. I had to make the conscious choice to control my mindset and attitude.

I had to focus on what I could control and let go of everything else. I controlled the controllables. My experience taught me that if I tried to control everything it would fracture my focus and diluted my efforts and outcomes so I only focused on a few things that I could control and thought were the most important and vital. Now I wasn't battling other bad guys. The new enemies were things like short cuts, temptations, distractions, cravings, and complacency. These are the enemies that will take you down.

I didn't know it at the time but back in Ghetto Village working with the dogs things started to change. As I was taking back control of my life, making the choices to do the things I wanted (and needed) to do, my thought processes were changing. I wanted to learn as much as I could about everything. I became curious about everything and started asking lots of questions! (The vets went crazy with all my why why why questions!). In hindsight, I would say I had a growth mindset. I put a priority on learning and growing. Why was this so important to me? It gave me a massive advantage over the smart, experienced, good looking, well connected others, many of who would never build these skills. They got by based on their other assets and didn't have to build these core skills.

From my experience, its all comes down to mindset. With this, you can learn everything else you need as you go along! Growth mindset is the corner stone of grit. Grit is the ability to set a goal and stick with it until it's complete. This ensures external elements don't dictate your outcomes.

What has always puzzled and intrigued me is why more don't choose! Why they don't empower themselves. We hear about so many that are in terrible relationships, or in a poor family situation yet they don't do anything to better themselves so they can get out of that situation. I can't understand it. They have the free will to choose and they don't exercise it? They make excuses or complain or justify the situation but they do nothing to get out of it. Don't be like that! Think about the future you want to have. Control your mindset and attitude. Take action. You have a choice, so choose! In the book "The Confidence Gap" by Russ Harris he states, "We can choose the pain of stagnation or the pain of growth. There is no such thing as a pain free life!"

Whose Attitude Is It Anyway?

It was another one of those hot humid July days in downtown Toronto in the mid 1980's. Today things were just unfolding in a nice mellow way. No rush, no hassles, just nice and easy. Life was good today. I was looking forward to the calm and coolness of the forest. Lady, Casy and I were going to High Park. They would run and chase the squirrels and finish up with a soak in the big fountain near the north entrance. I would enjoy their antics as cheap entertainment.

It was one of the classic older Toronto streetcars, a flat wine red colour on the bottom and a faded beige-tan colour on top. It had the pole running out back up to the wire on top for power. I could hear the clang clang of it coming down the rails and I could feel it shake the ground below my feet before it got to us. I was always a bit intimidated by these mammoths especially with my two dogs with me. My mind would think… what if we got in front of this thing? Splat! I would grip the leashes just a bit tighter.

We were taking the College 506 streetcar to High Park, aka "Squirrel City", so the dogs could run off leash. It was a fifteen-minute ride through Chinatown and then through some great old areas in the west end finishing up in High Park. This park is a wonderful gem in Toronto. Dense woods with walking trails, an animal petting zoo, a big pond, a few fountains, restaurant, an awesome kids play ground, a few sport fields all with a small road connecting them. High park is an amazing place for all.

On this day as we got on the streetcar it wasn't too busy so there were lots of empty seats near the back. I would often stand with the dogs near the rear doors as there was more space here and I could slide open the windows to get a breeze. All was calm. As we made our way down the aisle towards the back this Chinese women looked down and noticed the dogs. She exploded up, screaming in panic and waving her arms. She grabbed her child's hand, that looked to be about ten, and dragged her to make a quick exit from the streetcar through the middle doors. Wow, what was that all about? She obviously had negative experiences with dogs in her past. This got me thinking about how I thought about Chinese people as I had worked in a busy Chinese food restaurant for four years. Where did my beliefs come from? This led me to think about my beliefs and attitude towards anything. Where did they come from? Where they my own beliefs and attitudes or where they someone else's?

I've noticed that many adults who are afraid of dogs also have children who are afraid of dogs. This confuses me, as I have clearly seen many many times how most children are attracted to dogs, and puppies in particular. (They are so cute aren't they!) It's good to be cautious around dogs as they are animals and some can be unpredictable. It's altogether another thing to be deeply afraid to your core for no "learned" or justifiable reason other than your parents were afraid and instilled or "transferred" this fear in you. They implant their attitude and mindset to you.

When we are children our family and social environment instills core beliefs and limitations on us. However, as we get to be young adults and beyond, we become free to choose our own ways, our own beliefs and our own attitudes in life. We have to self-reflect and seek out those beliefs and attitudes that no longer serve us and replace them with more empowering and supporting ones. Our parents and caregivers mean well but we can't let other peoples limiting beliefs limit us.

My life experiences working with dogs has led me to understand that mindset, attitude and our philosophy towards life is what makes the biggest difference in the quality of our life. I saw this so clearly and learned how to apply this by working with dogs.

Taking the simple example of going for a walk. On any day, at any time, in any weather condition, just ask a dog if they want to go for a walk. Boom, they're up excited and ready to go. They have this unique ability to get excited over the simplest things. As the ancient wisdom goes, "Find joy in carrying water and chopping wood". Finding joy and even enthusiasm in the everyday "boring" tasks is what attitude is all about. And dogs have a great positive attitude.

Hindsight gives us clarity. It was like a hammer hitting me on the head, the realization that I can't change the world, but I can change me and how I respond to the world. I can work on changing my beliefs, my mindset, my perspective and philosophy on life. I could change the vision of myself and who I wanted to be and how I wanted to live. As the saying goes, life is 10% what happens to you and 90% how you choose to respond to it.

Dogs are pack animals. They like to have leaders, the alpha, which can lead and show them the way in uncertain times. In human speak these are our mentors, teachers, coaches, instructors, political leaders and so on. When we were children and young adults, we had our parents and the school system to help guide us. But what about now, as adults, who should we listen to and trust for advice and council?

Like the Romans, Egyptian's, tribal leaders, and leaders of countries, they all surround themselves with other trusted advisors that have synergistic knowledge in many focused and arrow areas. What do they know that we don't? Should we not surround ourselves with our own mentors and coaches, the trusted authorities who can lead, teach, inspire and help us build our skills more rapidly and effectively so we to can more easily deal with the hurdles and challenges life conjures up for us to overcome? Wouldn't this make our life easier, more fulfilling and enjoyable? I sometimes wonder how different my life would have been if I had had some of these trusted people around who I could rely on for good supporting information and guidance! I got "Go get your welding papers!" If we want more from our lives shouldn't we surround ourselves with mentors and trusted advisors?

I never asked for help, which in hindsight was foolish. If I had it would have greatly helped me get ahead and made things a lot easier for my forward progression. As well, I would have gotten the results I wanted a lot faster.

Dogs came into my life at a critical junction point and impacted where my future was going to go. Having dogs, learning how they simplify life and noticing how they go about living their days taught me the importance and power of mindset, attitude and philosophy. They helped me be more real and authentic to myself so my days became easier and more enjoyable.

Life can be tough so think about what Mark Twain said as you go though your day; "It's not the size of the dog in the fight, it's the size of the fight in the dog". As dogs have taught me, its all in your mindset, attitude and philosophy. It's time to get real.

LESSON 4
Being Authentic and Real

When I started working at the animal hospital in the early 1980's I just loved it. I loved the surgeries, I loved doing the lab work and x-rays, I loved the people and I loved all the different animals. But low and behold, they didn't all love me! These animals would be very real and authentic with how they were feeling about me.

It was a very clear message that would transcend all human and animal languages. There was no mistaking the clues and body language to what was being shared. It was very clear and succinct. The ears were down low and pulled back, the hair was sticking straight up on his back, and his tail was between his legs. And the clearest signal was the raised gums showing a well-developed set of large incisor teeth. What a set of chops this animal had.

We don't like everyone and not everyone likes us. That's life. On this day, this dog definitely didn't like me and was very open about it. He wasn't trying to protect my sensitive feelings. He would hurt me if I came into his space without feeling bad about it and he had no intention of keeping the peace. This dog was being very real and authentic with me. You threaten me, I don't like you, stay away or else I'll attack was the message. One of the wonderful traits dogs have is that of being authentic and real.

In a similar situation, most likely you've had a time when a dog came up to you wagging its tail or maybe its whole body and maybe they even jumped up on you because they were so happy to see you! Again, the message is very clear, they like you. And most likely you've been at a park with other dogs some of which come up, give you a quick smell then leave, signaling they aren't interested in you. Others stay as if to say they like you. They aren't thinking about you, they're thinking about what they like or don't like.

The dog park is such an incredible place to watch and see human and animal behaviour. People really seem to let their shells down and I've found they tend to be much more relaxed and authentic as they walk along and sip their coffee. I also find it revealing how their dogs sometimes mimic their attitudes and behaviour! I love to watch how the dogs play and interact.

Have you noticed that dogs don't get along with every other dog and they all seem cool with that? They don't worry that other dogs don't like them or what the other dogs think of them. They aren't trying to please you or make other dogs happy. And, they don't carry the baggage from yesterday forward and ruin today. They're guided by and march to their own drummer. They simply seek out those whom they get along with and hangout with them. They listen to their inner voice. They're true and authentic to themselves. What a blessing for us. If we hang out with them enough, this can rub off on us. This was true in my case.

Dogs really have the "simplify things" down. They tend to live and focus on a simple, uncluttered life; food, fun, friends, and sleep. There is no pretense in them. They are true and authentic. What you see is what you get. They don't bring yesterday's problems forward; they forgive, forget and move on. They aren't caught up in wants, they just zero in on their needs. They aren't getting caught up in what other dogs are doing or what they have. And they sure don't need all kinds of stuff they never use. They find contentment in what they have.

Another amazing trait is that they don't judge us based on our past, be it good or bad. They aren't thinking about whether you will be good to them today or mean to them tomorrow. They judge us based on our actions right now in the present moment. And very importantly, they don't build walls around their hearts to keep hurt out. Further still, most magnificently, they give openly and freely of love. They give you and me love unconditionally. They fully trust us and believe in us. Don't you agree, these dogs are the most wonderful animal companions? Thank goodness that they are so authentic and real. What you see is what you get with dogs.

Seeing how dogs acted, they were simple, very real and authentic, made me think about myself, and I started asking deeper questions of myself. Was I being real and authentic? Was I listening to my inner voice and following my own internal compass? I even started asking how can I be more in tune with my needs, desires and internal compass and really develop into the person who I wanted to be. Having dogs made me aware that I wasn't really being true to myself. I wasn't being the real me.

Who Are You?

There was something deep inside of me that knew it wasn't right. My belly brain was stirred. Maybe it was my conscious trying to tell me something. I thought I was doing a good job of hiding it; keep those who were innocent of my deeds at bay. I thought I was fooling some, but most likely I wasn't. I was only fooling myself and getting even more distant from the real me, my true and authentic self. Sneaking around in the drug culture always boozing and trying to hide what was going on in my life from others like my family members, certain friends, adults and the cops plays on your psyche. I would say it even makes you a bit paranoid and it definitely drives up anxiety and worry. It insidiously added to the force pushing away my connection to the real me. I wasn't real, I wasn't authentic and I wasn't being true to myself.

If my teen years in the 1970's were the dysfunctional and breakdown years then my twenties going though the 1980's were the discover and rebuild years. The early 1980's started off as an unsettling and transformational period for me though. There was an unsettling battle going on in my head and heart. I was starting to listen to my inner voice and use it as my guiding compass as I strained to navigate and grow towards the new me- who ever that was. Social pressures and the negative self-defeating internal dialogue were still alive and well, however my small positive steps forward were empowering and thus I was able to silence it somewhat. I was desperate to find or define the real me. I wanted to know who I actually was and what I was capable of. I kept digging to be more real and true to myself as that part of me was so far away from my reality. What do I want? What am I interested in? How do I want to fit into my social circle?

I loved being at the animal hospital as I was learning and growing so much. It was also an escape for me, but in a good way. As I was going though some major changes in my life it got me away from Ghetto Village. Working there was like therapy helping me get in touch with my deep inner wants and desires. I was being exposed to so many new and exciting things. It was helping me become more authentic and real to myself.

With my own dogs, to get them to like, listen and respond to me I was asking myself, how do I have to act? What behaviour's do I need to adopt for us to better get along and for them to respect and listen to me better? Do I need to be kinder, gentler, more patient, firmer, less angry and authoritative etc.? And, whom do I have to become for them to listen to and respect me? How can I earn respect from them so they listen to me?

How does this apply to people? If you're trying to attract the perfect mate, you may have a mental list of what you are looking for and want in that person. That's great to know what you want, but be cognizant that the other person probably has a list as well. Could you make it on their list? Would your characteristics, values, beliefs, actions and traits make it onto their "wish list"? If you want to attract that person, you could start asking who you have to become in character, body, mind, spirit and actions to attract them making sure to remain authentic to yourself.

Be True To You

This lesson of being authentic and true to oneself that I observed in dogs has been one of the most significant lessons I acquired and it has had a huge impact in my life. It's allowed me to accept who I am, to be happy in my own skin, to be happy with who I've become, and I've learned to love myself. What you see is what you get. But it wasn't easy or quick to get here.

It's hard to admit and to share, but I was in denial and I've noticed that many are as well. Many avoid the difficult truths in their lives. We become so busy that we don't have to hear the inner voices talking (crying out) to us. We become great experts at rationalizing and then shifting responsibilities away from ourselves onto others. We blame, complain and justify our situation instead of taking ownership.

At many of my workshops I would pose the question to the audience, how authentic are you? Right now if I asked you what your top five core values are, the true highest values that you live by, could you answer me? I'll give you the first three; family, health and finances, but not necessarily in that order. What are the others? Many didn't know what their values are and it's a great source of stress and "dis – ease". As the saying goes... If you don't know what you stand for, you will fall for anything!

Look at how this separation from our true self unfolds in our lives. After a while of putting your own needs, wishes, and desires on the back burner you start to lose touch with the real you, who you really are and what you really want and stand for. Simple things can act as a wedge; "Oh it doesn't matter, you choose where we eat", "I don't know, what do you want to do?" are some tiny examples. The separation gap slowly grows.

We may feel an unsettledness inside, then we start acting out in frustration, anger or resentment because we aren't living in alignment with our values and we aren't moving in the direction our heart wants us to move towards. We aren't doing the things we want to really do. Can you feel this? Does a little burning voice keep calling you to be or do things your way? Do you feel the itch or hear the voice to be something or someone else? I sure did. Is now the time to listen to it? If not now, when? When are you going to make the time to really listen to your heart and soul?

Many of us are trying to make others happy. We can be people pleasers. Are we doing things because they are the right things to do or because parents, friends, family, school, or the media wants us to do it instead of following our own direction and dreams? Are we living by our values or are we living by the values and judgments placed upon us by others in our society?

As I see it, most are being fed and digesting "junk values" from the mass media. We get separated from what we want and get bloated with these junk values so much so that we can't make decisions and move ahead with our lives. We can't decide on where to take our lives because we've lost touch with our own internal compass. Thus, I think it's important that we ask the question of what is it that we stand for? What turns our passion on or off? We need to get in tune with our inner compass. Ask ourselves the questions, what are we meant to be doing in this world? What are we good at? And importantly, what do we want to be good at?

Have you heard the saying the compass is more important than the clock? It's the understanding that it's better to know where you are going than how fast you're going! Take a look at how busy and stressed everyone is. They're going fast, but where are they going? Spinning away on the hamster wheel but not really getting any closer to what they truly and deeply want because they don't know. They've lost touch with their internal guiding light. Many are using retail therapy. We have to watch out for this. Getting caught up in a "constructive consumerism" mindset can be demoralizing and deadly.

Here is something to think about. Maybe you're going about your daily business doing "your" thing but you don't feel quite right. Something is off, missing or out of balance. Maybe you feel out of touch with yourself or you do something and then say, "Wow, that's not like me to do that". Your belly brain is talking to you, telling you something needs to change but you don't know what it is. You're not sad, but you're not happy either. You don't feel fulfilled with your job or maybe you don't feel emotionally connected in your relationships. You want more from life but you don't know what the more is! Think about this, maybe you're not actually doing "your" thing at all. Maybe you're just flowing along with all the other lost souls doing what society has plugged into your head? You're doing "their" thing!

We need to push back against these outside forces of "constructive consumerism" and stay true to ourselves. This is easy to say, but it's very tough to do if we don't know who we actually are or what we actually stand for or where we want to go.

It's easy to feel unhappy, unfulfilled or depressed when we are trying to achieve others or society's defined targets of success. And we'll probably burn out trying to hit them anyway. But more importantly, we won't be expressing, developing and growing into the real us. And sadly, after a while, we'll start losing touch with the real us as we become someone who we don't even recognize! At the end of our life, we all ask three common questions to ourselves; Did we live? Did we love? Did we matter?

When we aren't in tune with and not following our own internal compass, it's hard to make good decisions that reflect who we are, what we stand for and value. This creates a huge problem in our life. Most importantly, these key decisions impact where our life goes and the quality of our life; how fulfilled we are, how much satisfaction we have with our life, whether or not we have peace of mind and so on. When we are really in tune and living by our values and beliefs life gets much simpler and we get way happier! NICE! Again, look at dogs and how they live; true and authentic. And look at how happy they are!

Your Success

Another set of questions I would take people through at my workshops included questions around success. I would inquire; If I asked you what is your bulls-eye or the target your trying to hit or what does it mean for you to win and score, could you answer me? Another deeper question is, do you know what your purpose and mission are in your life? And further, how do you define success? Is it based on a financial number, accruing certain social cues and material goods (cars, houses, boats, clothes etc.)? Is it based on life experiences or family relationships and ties or maybe even the amount of personal growth or transformation you go through?

What was often reveled is that most are simply caught up in obtaining a financial number. Instead of wanting more, can we be happy with what we have and where we're at? It feels good to get the things we want in life, but are they the things *we* actually want? And, are we happy once we get them or is there always something more, something bigger and better that we are driven to get? As a thought, could you choose to be happier with less?

One core concept to living an authentic life came to me a bit later in life. I wish someone had told me this one much earlier. This understanding that no one seems to be talking about is the idea of success. Who's success are we talking about here? Yours, or the one that society and the media have plugged into our head that we think is ours? I'm talking about "constructive consumerism". This is the powerful marketing programs nudging us towards buying stuff that we don't really need or want and promoting this ideal of certain "perfect" people we should strive to be. To truly be happy and authentic, the question we should be asking to live life on our terms is "How do I define success?" The way I see it, success is not scarce that only a few get; it's abundant and all around us. And please understand, there is an abundance of it in our society, especially if you define it for yourself.

Others won't tell you this but the fact is, how we define success for ourselves determines if we are happy or miserable! Everyone needs to define his or her own version of success in the different areas of their life. This is where we need to be cautious. Don't define our success based on other people or the media's ideals of success. We need to change our perspective on what success is, define it for ourselves in all the areas of our life and go after it our way. The positive outcome is that this leads to peace of mind, freedom, as well as allowing us to be more authentic and true to ourselves. That's the ticket we're looking for.

How are you defining success? Is success for you having the big house, fancy cars and boats, expensive clothes, and the like? Is it having wonderful personal relationships and a rich family life? It is travelling and seeing the big wonderful planet we're on? Is it creating wonderful and creative paintings, sculptures, music or other artistic pieces that all of us get to enjoy? Is it standing up for a cause that is deeply close to your heart? What lights you up and gets you more interested and engaged in life? What do you need to do? Who do you need to become? What do you want your life to stand for? What is the legacy you want to leave? We all have a hunger to feel like our lives matter and we also want the things we do to matter as well.

Our personal growth is not static. I now understand that we are not **human beings,** we are **human becoming's**. Life is about becoming and moving towards the person who you want to be. This end goal will change over time and as we grow. So who are you becoming? Take the time now to write down your definition of success and be aware that it will change as you grow. To help you out with this, you can download the worksheet and fill it out from this website: https://healthsynergy.ca/bark/

Marketing is powerful. As I mentioned earlier, we may be living or following other people's ideas of who we should be, or living others or society's beliefs and living by their values. How do you know if you're doing this? Here is an easy test. Listen for the "should" word. Ask yourself, is this what I really want to do or is this what I *should* be doing? Reflect on why you do things, or when you make excuses for not doing them. Does the "should" word come up? Do you find yourself saying "yes I would like to do this or that but I *should* do this other thing over here?" Why do you think you're doing these "should" things? And who says you should do this or that? It's because of external pressures that we do them. Listen for this influence so we can silence it and get back into control.

Your Choices = Your Life

The quality of your life is based on the choices you make. If your choices are being influenced by external "should" pressures, then you aren't being true to yourself. Does it make sense to you that "should" are driven by external expectations and norms and that they are often not in alignment with what we really want to do? This leads to frustration, resentment, unsettledness and most importantly, it takes us away from being authentic and true to ourselves. Language can box us in and in a sense it can reduce our choices and freedom even though you think you have a choice.

A simple way I found to tap into our internal compass is to replace the word "should" with "could". This simple word change greatly reduces judgment of your choice; it reduces guilt around the choice and opens up many other possibilities. In a sense, it expands our freedom of what we really want to do. It allows us to get more in touch with our inner compass. It's empowering. And as a bonus, I know we will feel better around our decisions.

Whoa Robert, all this talk about values, beliefs, internal compass, and external forces is getting heavy. Absolutely it is. I have to call you out on this. If you don't know what your values are, if you don't know where you are going in your life, if you don't know how you define success, you can never obtain it and thus you are not being real and authentic to yourself. You're going to end up miserable, unfulfilled, resentful and most likely burned out. This doesn't seem like a good way to live the only life you have. Having dogs has lead me down this path exploring and discovering who I am and who I can be and now I want to help share it.

When we know where we're going in life, life becomes much simpler and our passion grows. If we live by our values and not someone else's, we have a much more rewarding life full of fulfillment and satisfaction with peace of mind. (You know the old wisdom; to thy own self be true). We can wake up energized and excited to take on the day because we planned it our way. We know we're going to do the things that give us a high amount of joy and purpose. That is super exciting! That's what being real and authentic to yourself is all about. Knowing who you are, what you stand for, what your values are and where you are taking your life. You can have a rich passionate life!

Working and being with dogs taught me that life is really simple; the quality of how you spend your time equals the quality of your life. Wasting our time equals wasting our life. Think about it, if we are consistently feeling stressed, out of control and overwhelmed how will this impact the quality of our daily life?

Good news though, if we value our time we value our life. This allows us to lead a life with joy, happiness, fulfillment, inner peace with purpose… so we live with passion. We can have control, feel relaxed and confident, and have peace of mind with inner peace. We can have direction, purpose and meaning in our life. It's not hard. We just need some guidance, direction and tools. And, we need to decide what we want. No one else can do this for us. We need to set aside some time to do the self-reflection required. Remember to live, love and matter! You can discover more on how to do this at this website: https://healthsynergy.ca/training-programs/

Having and being with dogs made me ask myself this question, so I ask again, how authentic are you? How real do you want to be? And more frankly, is this something that's even important to you? There is a growing body of research clearly showing that being authentic requires self-assessment and monitoring. As well, it's an ongoing process that requires us to connect to our inner voice and compass. Remember, we are human becoming's!

Don't be fooled by false connections. These days many appear to be connected to social media and the world via their devices, but they aren't that connected to themselves. One needs to quiet the outside distraction and listen closely to their inner voice. (I wrote about my challenge with this in lesson 4 on attitude and how is was so important for regaining back control of my life.) We may need to dissolve the beliefs and values we currently think are "ours" and replace them with more supporting empowering ones that actually are ours.

We need to quiet the voice that tells us what to do; the voice to be practical, conservative, safe and responsible and hear the voice that calls us. This is the voice of our spirit. We need to let go of the things that aren't important and have no meaning to us. We can build our lifestyle around the things that give us meaning and that we are passionate about. This will help lead us to happiness as meaning leads to happiness.

We have choices. We don't have to do this. Most won't. But then again, we will never really be facing our limiting beliefs and we will never get over the obstacles that are holding us back. My observation is that many have approach avoidance and stay stuck. Many justify or make excuses why they can't change. They blame others for their situation and may even take on a "victim" mentality; "poor me". Or worst still, is when they lower their standards and tell themself they didn't really want it (the goal) anyway. This leads to complacency and further erodes our self-trust and confidence. What a way to kill our spirit. What a way to "live".

Lets face our truths and realities. Lets become more authentic and true to ourselves. Surface, acknowledge and understand what our true philosophies and beliefs are as this will influence what we will and won't do and that impacts the results we get in our life. Our philosophies and beliefs determine the quality of our life. To help you with this you can download the worksheet to understand and build more supporting and empowering beliefs. You can download the worksheets from this website: https://healthsynergy.ca/bark/

What we should think about is honest self-assessment, which means self-reflecting and being our own counselor. It allows us to develop our own views and it helps us to define who we want to be in character and actions. It helps cultivate our innate ability to more closely examine who we are so you can think objectively through our problems or challenges. It helps us become more authentic and real to others and ourselves. Assessing our strengths and weaknesses can encourage us to get mentoring or coaching to build ourselves up and have more balance.

However, true self-assessment is difficult to do thus I would suggest we surround ourselves with trusted friends and mentors who will be honest and call it like it is with us about our actions, and results. (Even good friends may not be able to really "tell it like it is" to us. They won't want to hurt our feelings.) Mentors and coaches can also help share insights on the areas that we might need the most improvement in our life. My advice is to listen to them and listen to yourself.

I met a nice guy who mentioned he didn't like going to the dog park. I asked him why not? He stated, "Other dogs seem to keep wanting to fight with my dog". I simply replied, "Maybe it's not the other dogs. You might want to take a look at your dog's actions and behaviour to see if he's provoking them." He looked at me like I was from Mars and moved away from me. I get it. We all know our own dogs are all sweet little angels and would never do something like provoking fights. We might want to take a deeper look at what is really going on in them and ourselves.

This same sort of thing applies in our own life. Consider your own actions before pointing the finger at others. If you are having multiple challenges or failures it's in our human nature to blame the circumstances or other people or the fairness of the universe for the problem. Truth be told though, we need to step back and ask a tough question, and it's hard to do… Is it me? Am I the problem here? People's reactions are reactions to us. They are reflecting and "mirroring" us and our energy. What vibe are we giving the world? If we want people around us to change, change the image we have in the mirror. Do what Michael Jackson sang; "I'm starting with the man in the mirror. I'm asking him to change his ways. And no message could have been any clearer; if you wanna make the world a better place; take a look at yourself and then make a change." This is simple and very powerful advice for all of us.

Your Definition Of You

You can remove the parking brake to your forward progression and make your life easier. We can tease out what's holding us back by looking at how we describe ourselves. Why is this important? Our identity is nothing but a definition of ourselves. With a definition comes parameters, boundaries and rules on how we should act and be. This in turn impacts what we will or will not do, (that's our behaviour) and the actions we take or don't take. And here is a vital key point to really understand, our behaviour will be congruent and support our identity (be it a positive or negative identity). This leads to the results we have in our lives! As a very simple example, we all do dumb things from time to time and we might even say "that was a dumb thing to do". But there is a big difference from this and the belief where you say to yourself; I'm dumb! Strange as it may seem, we will end up doing dumb things just to prove our belief right.

Using the example from my own life as I wrote about previously, I started to believe that I was a slow learner, a dummy, a loser, trouble, a druggie, an "A-hole", worthless etc. That was my belief because so many called me those names for so long. I believed them! And because I believed them, I was acting in ways to be congruent with the definition of those labels. This wasn't on purpose; this was running in the background, this was my subconscious at work. Adding in the fact that I was sneaking around try to hide my negative actions and behaviour related to drugs and boozing, I was so out of touch and distant from who I was and wanted to be.

It wasn't until I started taking back control and purposefully redefining who I was and who I wanted to be and acted in the ways to support that belief that things dramatically changed for me. I redefined how I defined myself and what I wanted to believe about myself. I started to live into this new belief. It was a slow and very tough process for me though, I had so much self-doubt, but I slowly did it. And you can to. The great news for you though, it will be much faster for you to travel down this path as you now know the strategy on how to make it happen.

The important insight to understand is that most of the time we are not aware of how we describe ourselves. Thus, we have hidden limits on our forward progression because of these descriptions and beliefs. And the rotten part is, we don't even know it. We end up frustrated and unfulfilled. To be more true and authentic to ourselves it's vital to become more aware and conscious of how we identify ourselves and the beliefs that go with these labels. Good news though, once we understand this and start taking control of how we describe ourselves, life can dramatically change! To help you with this, you can use the insights worksheet at this link. You can also watch the training videos I made for you on this and other topics covered in the book. https://healthsynergy.ca/bark/

The ability to have a heart to heart, truthful discussion with yourself is important for becoming more authentic. Step back and disengage to get the birds eye view of the situation. This new perspective can be critical in determining whether or not your choices and actions are helping or hindering your forward progression.

Being true to yourself and being more deeply authentic is part of living a meaningful life, which in turn leads to greater happiness. Being truly authentic comes down to trust. We need to ask, am I being truthful about who I am? Do you ever question some of your actions and think; Whoa, that wasn't like me, why did I do that? Was I trying to be cool? Did I feel outside pressure to be that way? Ultimately only you will know so it's important to be in touch with the driving forces of your behaviour.

Connecting back to the "perfect" Facebook post so many put up, are we comfortable not being perfect in the eyes of others for fear of being judged? Are we comfortable sharing our failures and weaknesses? Being honest like this helps us be perceived as more genuine and real which in turn builds more trust, which as you know is key in all relationships. Through my life I've learned to embrace more of my quirks and uniqueness. They are turning out to be some of my biggest strengths. I'm turning my troubles into treasures! My mind is often going a mile a minute and runs off on many different tangents. I'm always coming up with new ideas and plans and this makes it hard for me to stay on task and focus. However, on the treasure side, I get all kinds of ideas and am great at brainstorming. This helps me in my work to come up with new strategic solutions and with my creative hobbies to produce new ideas. What a gift!

To help you cultivate authenticity here is a simple sentence completing task. On a piece of paper write out the question, "If I were going to be 5 percent more authentic, I would _____ ". Do this multiple times and try to really drill down to the ways you can be more true to yourself. Then, act on them. Do these things.

Another way to think about being authentic is that ultimately it doesn't matter who is around us, we are our own constant companions so we have to please ourselves and like our own company. So if we aren't completely happy with where we are at, do something about it. We now know what to do. Grow ourselves into the person we want to become, and enjoy the company!

Many are aware that in biology there is talk of homeostasis, a steady state that is reached where things stay the same. In reality though, this is not the case with living systems. There is always movement and change. There is always flux and things are never static. We call this homeodynamics, which means constant change. This happens in all systems and in our lives. We are either growing or we are dying in our physical health, mental health, emotional health, spiritual health, in our finances and so on.

Take Back Control Of You

Here is a simple fact of our modern life, either we proactively define ourselves or external forces (family, friends, work, the media, society etc.) will do it for us. We are responsible for our own happiness. Our life is a result of the choices we make. If you don't like your life, it's time to start making better choices. Choose to be the person you truly want to "BE". Remember, we are human becoming's!

I've always been one to find the positive, the good and the humour in things and situations even though my childhood and teenage years had some extreme events in them. Is this due to genetics or survival instincts? I don't know the answer to that question but I do know that trying to get ahead in life, living life to the fullest isn't easy when we are always negative and just floating down the river of life without direction, purpose, mission or vision of where we are going. It's hard to push back and fight for what we want when we don't know what it is we're fighting for. And, it's hard to be energized when we have no internal motivation and meaning to drive us forward in our life.

Not honestly knowing what our true values are or living by them leads to an unfulfilled life of "blah". There is no real vibrancy or enthusiasm for living, no peace of mind, and little sense of accomplishment. It leads to a life without any real passion. As the saying goes "if you don't know what you stand for, you'll fall for anything!" YUCK!

I've been asking myself more and more… what's most important at the end? Would I have any regrets? Did I live a full life? Did I live by my values and achieve my most important goals? Did I live an authentic life and did I live with passion? Did I love openly without holding back or without being overly protective of my heart? Have I mattered? Have I made a difference in a positive way in the world and left it a bit better than when I arrived? Do you ever have these thoughts?

Death has a way of focusing your attention and gets you to evaluate your life. Having being exposed to many deaths through the 1980's from those at the animal hospital as well as having my brother in law and my own youngest brother die tragically and unexpectedly, to the loss of both grandparents has more than ever made me re-evaluate my values, my goals and mission in life to help me get an even clearer vision of where I want to go. And it's allowed me to be much more authentic to myself. More good news, you can have this too without going thought all this emotional upheaval. Thank god (dog spelt backwards) again!

Be - Do - Have Exercise

Do you want to know a super fast and easy way to get more direction in your life so you have more purpose and direction? How about an easy way to tune into your values? If so, do this fun exercise now. Get three pieces of paper and on the top of one write the word "BE", on one write "DO" and on the last write "HAVE". This is the "be, do have" exercise. It's fast and easy to do. This can be even more fun if you do it with a partner. You can download the sheets here: https://healthsynergy.ca/bark/

Now start with the "have" one first. I want you to just brainstorm and write or type as fast as your thoughts come to you all the stuff you want to "have" in your life. This is actually fun to do. Go for it now! No holds barred. List everything and be extreme if you want, we won't judge you. If possible, prioritize your list with things you want to have quickly versus longer-term wants.

Next, write all the things you want to "do" in your life. Where you want to travel, things you want to see, and accomplish. Again, prioritize your list. Heads up, this may be a bit harder and require some deeper thought. It's fun to do as well. These first two pages will help you complete your bucket list of things you want in your life.

Now, the most interesting one is last. The "BE" list. Who do you want to be in person, in spirit, in character, and in action? How do you want to describe yourself? What traits would you want friends and family to say you were? Would you want to be kinder, more passionate, less shy, happier, more authentic, more expressive and so on. This one will require some deeper thought. You may find it very easy or very difficult to do. Once you are done, prioritize which trait you want to work on first, second etc. Here is a link to a document you can download with many different virtues, emotions etc. on it to help stir your own creative juices. https://healthsynergy.ca/bark/

I don't want you to get stressed out over this. You don't have to finish all this in one sitting but get the bulk of it done soon. Now, sit back and look at what you've created. You now have a plan of what you want in your life. A list of what you want to do and who you want to BE all in a prioritized list. This is your current road map to fulfillment, authenticity and happiness. Again, remember, this will evolve with you over time.

Here is a powerful understanding that might give you goose bumps. Humans are amazing creatures. The front of our brains (the frontal lobes) allow for "forethought" which allows us to visualize the future. You can "see" into the future and visualize what you want it to be. Here is the amazing part, as a human you can now write the next chapter of your life and how you want to live and BE and then live into it. You have your own personal plan in your hand. How amazing is this!

Start going through your list and "Be, Do, Have" the things that will make your life amazing for you. You may poo poo this exercise and say "nah, this is hokey", this is too simple and you are right, it is simple. But boy oh boy, it is oh so powerful and functional. Set aside an evening and do this. This simple little exercise changes everything!

Sometimes things happen in life that make us think the world in collapsing in on us. We need ways to see through the darkness. To help pull ourselves up when we are down. Learning to see the good, looking and finding the positive and knowing what you want and living by your values quickly helps put things into perspective and that is empowering. And when overwhelmed, you have direction and purpose to allow you to focus and pull you through. Cool!

No matter how many mistakes you make or how slow your progress, you are still way ahead of everyone else who isn't trying and has no focus. Think about this, a sixty watt light bulb can light up a room but its effects diminish rather quickly from its center. Take the same power, sixty watts, and turn it into a laser beam. With this laser you can hit the moon! Can you grasp the power of having focus and direction and how powerful this strategy is? This could be a life changer for you.

If you want to go one step further and really help make the shift to the new you and really get into living the way you want to BE, you can add a bit more clarity to your self-definition by reviewing the list of values and virtues and chose the ones that you want to use to describe you.

Here is another empowering exercise you can do to get deeper clarity on how you want to BE. You can go over the list of values and virtues and find the words you would like to use to describe yourself i.e. honorable, spirited, authentic, thoughtful, bold, dependable, loving etc. and come up with 3 words you want to use to describe yourself in business situations and 3 words you want to use to describe yourself in social situations.

OK, you now have the words that you want to describe yourself with. To drive these words into your subconscious you need to consistently remind yourself of how you want to "BE", so after a while it becomes a habit and they are deep in your mind. One easy way to make this happen is every time you go through a door or door frame use it as a trigger to set your memory into motion to bring up these key words. Then repeat them a few times to yourself and get into "character"... BE!

Another way is to set your phone with an alarm 3 or 4 times per day to remind yourself how to BE. You could even go old school and use those post it notes and put them by your computer, in your car, on your mirror or fridge etc. You get the idea.

Being with dogs for many years has allowed me to observe their behaviour and in my own simple ways tease out what I think makes them happy and apply the lessons to my life to enhance my happiness. Living a simpler life and being true and authentic to ones self is one key life lesson that has helped me tremendously. My life is more fulfilling and I have contentment with peace of mind. I still set large goals and work towards making my other dreams come true but the good news is... I do it my way! I'm a human becoming and so are you! This can be another great reason for having dogs in your life.

Just like how a lobster or a snake has to shed its outside skin to allow them to continue to grow we may have to shed some relationships and definitions of ourselves to grow. So I ask, is there a part of your self-definition or a belief you have about yourself that you may need to let go to make room for the new you? Does this generate a bit of worry? If you feel stressed and overwhelmed with life, can you see how simplifying and living by your true values would give you a greater peace of mind and fulfillment? What is one action step you can take towards this today? Go do it. And take your dog.

I truly believe that having dogs in my life guided me down a new path and gave me a new direction in life. Seeing how they behaved and how real and authentic they were made me evaluate me! I wanted to get in touch with the core and essence of the real me, of who I really was. My life had drifted far from this vision. I wanted to be more authentic and real. Having dogs around makes one more real and authentic not only to yourself but to others as well. I can't believe how fortunate I was to have them come into my life and for this I'm forever grateful. If you are reading this I know you must feel the same. How lucky are we! Thank goodness for dogs!

For fun, think about this; if you could be a dog, what kind of dog would you want to be? How would you act and who would your other doggie friends be? Interesting questions aren't they. I hope this gives you some insights and direction into your real, true authentic self.

By removing distractions and simplifying our lives we can gain further clarity on who we are and get that much closer to being more authentic and real. This is another great life lesson I learned from dogs the ability to simplify

LESSON 5
Simplify

All my dogs loved going to the dog park but Max was by far the most social one. He worked the crowd like nothing I've ever seen before. Going from person to person and dog to dog. He wanted to see everyone and say "Hi". He also liked his quiet times when he need time to be alone to do his dog thing. This was one of those times.

Back and forth, back and forth. He kept repeating this movement. Grabbing it, a few quick chews, dropping it, grabbing the other one with some more quick chews, digging his teeth into it then repeat. This was an important assessment. I could literally see his little brain working overtime trying to decide what one he wanted the most. He must have been thinking, "Which one would the other dogs want the most!" or "Which one would show them I'm the most dominant or strongest?" Or simply, "Which one tastes the best!" The bigger, thicker and much longer dried out one or the slimy, short chunky one with the branches still on it. It was almost painful to watch. I was yelling to myself, "Come on and choose already".

Finally he dragged the bigger stick off the trail, flopped down and dug into a good chew session! You could read the happiness and pleasure on his face. Wow, all this fuss over a stick! It was an important decision. He knew he couldn't have both so he chose the one most important to him, the one that was going to make him feel the best and went for it. This was another great lesson for me. Simplify and slow down life like a dog's life. It's elementary really; decide exactly what you want, remove all the other things that get in the way of achieving it, and then take action to get it. This is an ancient concept.

"Life is really simple, but we insist on making it more complicated" is an old quote from Confucius. Life has always been busy for everyone and thus to achieve greater happiness it's the mental strength to push back to the busyness of the day. We need to draw the line in the sand and commit to living a simpler and thus happier life. It's about resisting the marketing and advertising (constructive consumerism) that keeps telling us we need more of the latest and greatest things to be happy and that without them we won't be fully actualized.

Maybe it was from growing up without much stuff or from all the time I've spent working with dogs, but it seems to me that most of the things that improve our lives don't have to be complicated. There are no magic recipes to discover. The ingredients aren't magical, hidden or impractical and they aren't secret. Further, they don't require a great investment of resources. Rather, the core fundamental building blocks of a happy and fulfilling life are simple and straightforward. Humans have known about them for a very long time. Eat nurturing foods, exercise and move, visit with friends and socialize, spend time in nature, build positive memories based on your experiences, reduce negative relationships, give more love and improve yourself. These seem to be the key fundaments I've learned from dogs on how to live a great life. Simplify and focus on the really important stuff. But this doesn't seem like it's applied in our society and daily living.

Keeping It Simple Is Smart

Many of us have homes and garages filled with "stuff" we never use and maybe even trip over to get to the few things we use all the time. There is a great book called "Stuffocation" written by James Wallman that describes how this has developed. For most of us, what have we filled our rooms with? How big is our closet and how full of clothes is it (most of which are from 20 years ago) and when exactly are you planning on wearing them again?

My observation is that we need to remove the unimportant clutter and the distractions that get in the way of us having and doing the things that are of most importance to us. Basically, removing all barriers to forward progression and happiness. How can we be happier with our life? I might suggest simplifying it.

In the movie "The Minimalist" and in the bestselling book entitled "The Life -Changing Magic of Tidying up" the common theme is about getting rid of the clutter and distractions so you can focus on the vital and important. In essence, everything we have should give us warm and fuzzy feelings and bring joy into our life. Having stuff just for the sake of filling space has never been a good idea. We need to dial things back and get rid of the frenzy mentality of buy, buy, buy. It's so draining. We need to resist and push back to regain control of our true values and wants.

Instead of always trying to get more, what would happen if we focused on simplifying, decluttering and being happier with what we have? Or even better, could we learn how to be happier with less! What a concept. (Does it send fear down your back just thinking about this?) In how many awesome ways would we feel freed up and even liberated with the removal of this extra baggage? By the way, there is definitely a trend towards this. Dogs have known this for a long time. Less can be more!

Time equals life. If we waste our time then we waste our life. We can't have and do it all. We can't have and be all those things the big marketing companies tell us we need. We just don't have enough time. Thus you have to choose what's most important to you. You have to decide what your deepest, truest values are, the things that give you the greatest pleasure and meaning in your life. Don't live by someone else's values and beliefs. What are the "rules" that you will live by and stand by that act as your internal compass? You need to live by them. Like my dog Max, what stick is going to be the juiciest for you?

With so many choices and things to do in life we will always have to make choices and compromise. As you now understand, it comes down to knowing what we truly value and truly want. It's about what are we willing to give up to get what we really want. What is it that has such high value to you that you are willing to sacrifice something else to have it? And then be good with your choice. I think we have to make smarter and informed compromises to have a more fulfilling life. To do this we have to be in touch with what we really want (not what the marketers have programmed us to want) so we choose carefully and don't waste so much time and energy on the wrong things. Steven Covey has a famous quote, "Most people spend their whole lives climbing the ladder of success only to realize, when they get to the top, the ladder has been leaning against the wrong wall." This can be followed by another one of his quotes, "If the ladder is not leaning against the right wall, every step we take just gets us to the wrong place faster." How sad would that be to live that life? Thus you can now recognize the importance of simplifying and focusing on the right things for you?

Doing something exceptionally well means we will have to give up things in other areas of life. We have to let them go. We can't have it all and do it all. But we can have what we deeply and truly want if we simplify and focus. We will always have to compromise, thus it's about what are we willing to give up to get what we want? We can make smart, informed compromises. Smart decision-making is key. And simplifying makes it easier.

If we are letting something go or "sacrificing" to get something of greater value to us we have to be ok with the choice. We have to be cool with the sacrifice and not have regrets or remorse. There is something called buyers remorse. This is when you buy something and then think, oh, should I have gotten this or the other one, did I pay too much, and will it be cheaper somewhere else? It's doubt that we didn't make the right decision. We don't need more doubt in our lives, it robs us of our confidence.

I've noticed that many, including myself, get caught up with over analyzing things. I fill my brain with so many facts and logic that emotion is totally left out of the equation thus when I finally do make a decision it isn't always as rewarding and fulfilling as I was hoping for. I don't get the emotional pleasure from my choice. I keep thinking, what if … the other choice! I would now suggest keeping emotion in the buying equation so you have a deeper sense of satisfaction with your purchase. You'll feel better about it.

Another great way to reduce the agony of indecision is by asking yourself two questions about your choice. After you decide, would you say to yourself "I wish I didn't do X" or "I'm glad I did Y"? This is a simple way to get to the root of the decision. And the good news is, once you decide, the agony and doubt you were experiencing will go away!

Make The Decision Right

To further help simplify your decision making and reduce your stress, empower yourself and ask some new questions; Did I make the right decision vs. can I make this decision right? My life experiences have instilled the understanding that if you are on the fence and indecisive about a choice, simply choose one and don't worry about if it's the right decision. Optimize your thinking and tell yourself how can I make my decision right! And completely let the other one go. No regrets or remorse. This simple way of looking at decisions will remove much mental stress and anxiety.

Further to this idea of making decisions is the notion of taking on and accomplishing new challenges to keep growing. Sometimes we won't be certain of what to do and we get stuck by over analysis. A new way to think about this might be to stop thinking about what you need to do or what is the right thing to do, rather, change your focus and mindset and ask yourself a new empowering question; "Who do I need to become?" Which one of these decisions would best contribute to my growth of that ideal?

Start acting like the person you are trying to become. If you want to lose weight, ask yourself, what would a fit person eat right now, how would they move or exercise? If you wanted to be a better husband or wife ask yourself, how would they act, what would their attitude be, what are some of the key actions they would take and then do them! Focus on who you need to be in body, mind, attitude and spirit.

I heard a person named Joshua Becker speaking on simplification and he summed up this lesson I learned from dogs nicely. "Minimalism for me is the intentional promotion of the things we most value and the removal of anything that distracts us from it. While there is certainly some overlap with decluttering, minimalism takes a harder look at possessions. Decluttering is typically considered as removing "clutter" from our living spaces, but minimalism asks a further question: What do I actually need to fulfill my purpose in life? And how can I remove everything else permanently?" Nice! That's what I see dogs do. They go after the core fundamental things that make them happy and then let go and forget everything else.

"At the End of My Leash" was an aptly named TV show we would watch with our two children when we first got Max. I wanted them to develop the understanding of how dogs think and how to interact with them in more appropriate ways as we were training Max. We wanted to empower them with the skills to better bond with Max who was officially "their dog". The star of the show was Brad Pattison who is a dog behaviour trainer and human life coach.

Brad would go into people's homes to help train the dogs of "bad" behaviour. When they went into this particular home they found the owners had purchased over ten different beds for the dog, had hundreds of chew toys, thirty plus outfits and all kinds of other paraphernalia for the dog. Really? What were these people thinking? And even with all this stuff, the dog still wasn't happy and behaving "right". The solution? Get rid of all this stuff and take the dog on two good long walks per day! Simplify and focus on the basics. What do you really need to be happy? I might suggest simplifying.

As I learned from dogs, possessions don't make us happy and as a matter of fact, they can be a burden. By pushing back against consumerism we are getting rid of external motivators. This in turn allows us to nurture and develop our true internal drives and motivators. This will help make us feel more authentic and gives us that all-important direction in life.

There is a huge amount of abundance in our life coinciding with a mentality of buy, buy, buy. However I would ask, do we need more stuff or do we need more direction and meaning in our life? By getting rid of clutter and distractions we can calm down and quench this imposed never being satisfied drive to buy. If you really want to get to the next level in your life, if you truly want to "fly" then you need to get rid of all the things that weigh you down and hold you back. Simplifying can help you do this.

Have you heard of the Tiny Home movement? People are forgoing their larger more modest homes and choosing to live in much smaller spaces, some as small as 250 square feet. This forces them to choose the few truly necessary possessions to live with. It cuts all the fat if you will from the true core of what they need to live. And it makes them really value and appreciate what they end up keeping. It's also interesting to note that most of these folks comment on how much happier they are in these new spaces. A smaller space, less "stuff" and yet they're happier. Go figure. This is something interesting to consider in our lives.

In architecture, there is a trend in cities to building "micro" condos. These are apartment style condos with very small spaces of 350 square feet or so. The architect and designers then will take a floor of the building and turn it into a common living room that the tenants can go to too socialize. Many were asking, "Why do we all need space that most of us never use? If we are going to relax and lounge, why not do it together?" Again the idea of quality over quantity space is examined.

One of the things that stresses people out is the feeling of being overwhelmed. Reducing our stuff reduces the distractions they have on us. It's these distractions that keep us away from what we really want to do. This comes back to regaining control of your life. As I shared from my life when I was teen and young adult, I had to focus on a few things that I could do right and well to counter all the negatives that were in my life. I desperately need to regain control of my downward spiraling life. These were the things that I discovered and knew would move me ahead in my life. I couldn't afford distractions. Their "cost" would have been too great to bear.

Having and working with dogs taught me the importance of simplifying so I could focus on my real priorities and live closer to my truest values. It allowed me a greater sense of sustained joy and happiness. It helped reduce the overwhelm I felt and it kept me humble. And as a side benefit, as I was often moving, it made the moves much easier with less stuff.

Simplifying is not just about having fewer possessions; it's about living more simply in general. It's about removing the distractions and anything that is keeping us from fulfilling our greater purpose in life. Please remember, these principles can be applied to our health, our schedules, our relationships, our online worlds, and even the words we use when we speak.

How much better would we feel if we helped others out and got rid of the extra clutter and stuff in our homes? We could donate all this stuff to charities or those who have less. How great would that be? Help yourself by helping others. Remember the old saying, "One person's trash is another person's treasure".

And finally, think about how truly amazing it would be to get rid of all that extra clutter and stuff in the garage so you could actually park the car in it at night! How good would that be! For more inspiration, go take the dog for a walk. Things will clarify in your mind when you're out with them. Simplify.

When you are on your walk, watch how you dog interacts and socializes with the other four-legged animals. See how they behave and play with the other dogs. Do they perk up and get excited, who do they chose to play and hang out with, do they play with some and then let them drift way to focus on other dogs, do they act all dominant or are they submissive and shy? Watch closely. Social connections are one of the keys to longevity and happiness and dogs are great at it. What can we learn from them?

LESSON 6
Social Connection's

As we didn't have "dog parks" in the early 1980s we all just took our dogs to the local parks. Where I lived in north Don Mills it was suburban heaven and thus there were lots of green belts between the backyards of the houses. These were wonderful for walking your dog, as it was mostly fenced on both sides for a few kilometers. They often were lined with trees, shrubs and other plants backing onto the greenbelt from some of the homes. You could walk almost carefree as the dogs ran, played and did their business. They were perfect and many walked their dogs here. Sometimes even the public schools play areas would open up to and connect with the greenbelts. The greenbelts were the socializing spots and these playgrounds were the training grounds for the dogs.

It was very exciting times for them, the highlight of their day. Sometimes Lady and Casy both would start to shake. Often Casy would start into a deep howl of happiness as we approached the parking lot. To be honest, it was kind of embarrassing. And me, being the over bearing disciplinarian I would always make them sit still and quiet before they exploded from the car. I wanted them to have some self-control, my new mantra. The dogs knew playtime was here and they were excited. The dogs were great one on one, however, it was always so uplifting to see how they would come alive in new ways when they met with their doggy friends at the park.

Who and how they played with was always interesting to me. Some loved to chase, and others loved to be chased. These ones always found each other, just like humans do! Others wanted to fetch or to play tug-o-war. And I got to socialize as I met some other dog owners.

We have all heard the story about the lone wolf going alone and making it happen. There is something majestic about this idealist picture. Fact is though, dogs are very social beings and do best when they are with others. Their hunting success, reproduction and survival rate is better in a group. And I believe, so is their happiness. My simple observations over my life would confirm this thought. Dogs are good on their own with humans, but they thrive with other dogs. Maybe you've seen this in your own dog as well.

The old saying, when the student is ready, the teacher will appear rang true. There was no big "Ah Ha" moment but the pattern was clear, Lady and Casy were always happier when they were playing and socializing with other dogs. It dawned upon me, maybe I needed to get out and socialize more. I had severed many of the ties with my parting friends and now missed the company. Maybe I needed to relax and see some old friends! Duh! As the poetic words in the song "Hollywood Nights" by Bob Seger reveal, "See some old friends, it's good for the soul". If you ever need an excuse to get out and socialize this is it! This type of "socializing medicine" can be a potent elixir to lift the spirits, reduce loneliness, boost a positive outlook on the world as well as make you happier. And maybe even live longer! Nice!

It's a simple lesson but very pertinent in our modern highly connected world. Yes it's nice to text, email or Snapchat someone to connect but we aren't always truly present. There is much more going on with our relationships that require more than a text to satisfy. Both the physical aspect and the emotional aspect need nurturing. And you've felt it. When you go out with friends or meet at a gathering we always feel better and uplifted with others. It's nice to see people's reaction to news or see their mannerism and gestures that add so much to the experience and communication. And, we can say more and clarify things if a wrong message is transferred. And it's easier on our thumbs! The same is true with our dogs. They love to socialize as well.

Socialization
Our last family dog, Max, came into our lives at the end of 2010. The kids had picked him out of the litter, or maybe he picked them! In hindsight, we should have called him Casanova. He had long golden fur with tuffs of white that would get curly in the warm air, kind of like he had a perm. And his fur was very soft. His ears would bounce up and down like little wings as he ran. His tail would stick

straight out the back like a flag with the white tuffs hanging down waving in the wind. He would steal you heart with his charming good looks. It wasn't his physical size that made the impact, as he was only about 35 pounds, rather it was his demeanor and character that announced his presence. Max was the King of socializing.

Max was a very happy-go-lucky kind of dog. He liked everyone and everyone liked him. He could work a room and lift everyone's spirits like nothing I've ever seen before. And for himself, he was happy and content running in the woods tracking scents of other little critters. Enlightening for me though, it was amazing to see him shift gears and become almost giddy with joy when he saw his other doggie friends at the park. It was truly amazing how he took it to the next level.

Dogs don't seem to need others to make them happy. Yes they are definitely happier when they get to play and socialize with their doggie friends as they are very social creatures, but they don't need the extrinsic factors or stimulus to be happy. They can be content and happy just by being. This is internal or intrinsic happiness.

Humans are also highly social beings. We can be happy and content by ourselves as well. Most would comment though that we are better and happier with others. And this is supported by research. The greatest predictor of happiness and success is social connections. The breath, depth and meaning of the connections are very important. If success and happiness is just about you there is a limit/ cap on it, and it's hard to sustain it. To remove the cap and to sustain happiness longer we need to help others feel better and be happy as well. At this point the cap comes off and you can sustain the happiness longer. We truly are better together!

Current insights revealed from positive psychology show that humans do best and thrive when in social groups. As a matter of fact, in his books The Happiness Advantage and BIG Potential, Sean Anchor presents the case that we need social groups to be truly happy. He goes on further to state that social networks are key to our happiness. This idea was explored even farther in the book Blue Zone of Happiness, by Dan Buettner, who came up with similar conclusions; social interactions are key to our happiness.

Yet what is happening in our busy and stressed world? When we get stressed, instead of doing something that may nourish us, we do the opposite, we withdrawal and retreat to isolation. Sean Anchor suggests that when we are stressed, instead of retreating to isolation, it's best to go find your friends and interact with them in a social setting and invest in your social network.

Have you experienced this? I did when I went back to high school when I was twenty. I thought I was content by myself but I was wrong. I had unknowing slowly started isolating myself from others. Time was tight. I had taken on two more jobs over and above working at the animal hospital. I was working for the city of Toronto's Parks and Recreation department during the days and delivering Chinese food at night. I was always working, studying, walking the dogs or reducing stress by working out. Most of the time I was alone. This was very different from my previous life where I was always partying and socializing with others all the time. When I got to university with its greater demands for study time things got worse still. I was slowly slipping into a mild depression because of this social "isolation".

Stepping back and isolating ourselves whether by accident or on purpose can play a role in building a wall to keep out the hurt of lost love but it can also act to keep out the one thing most of us want and need more of, love. Seeking others and socializing more can help to disassemble this wall and let more love and happiness find us. This is a wonderful benefit of having dogs; they can get you out with others and boost your happiness. I wrote more on this in the chapter on love.

As food for thought, a key predictor of longevity is also our social connections. If you want to live longer, data from Dan Buettner's first book "The Blue Zones" shows that a key to living a longer and happier life is social connections! So if social connections are the best predictor of happiness, what can we do with this knowledge? Build our social connections of course. This is synergy. You can add joy to others lives and lift them up and they can in turn boost your joy and happiness. And take your dog with you. That way, everyone wins!

I never did organized team sports when I was a boy. And as a good o' Canadian boy I should have been playing ice hockey but I didn't. Most of the physical activities I've done have been individual events; running, motocross, triathlons, and cycling. It wasn't until around age fifty when I started to play hockey. I wasn't very good but I found I loved the game and wished I had started playing earlier in my life. I learned how rewarding it could be to set others up to win and share the success of a good play and goal. I was also very surprised at how forthcoming other players were to help coach me to improve and get better. It was in their best interest of course if I was on their team. With hockey, I don't go and workout or exercise hockey, I go and "play" hockey. I'm still not very good but I truly love the comradely of the teams and the socialization.

The commonality of the love of the game is a real social equalizer. I play with professors, doctors, musicians, trades people, truck drivers, a fire fighter, physiotherapist, chiropractors and many others. We aren't judging each other on our social status, it's how good of a player are you! There is lots of banter about the game, how we played, current events, our wives and kids and of course our aches and pains. It always lifts my spirits when I play and it's due to the socializing, the connection and bonding. And this is also true at the dog park.

The Dog Park

If you have a dog you've been there. The place where dogs run free, balls are thrown, sticks are tossed, coffee is sipped, stories shared, butts are sniffed, and poop is scooped. It's the dog park. Both parties, the dogs and the people, get excited about going. With Max I usually went to the dog park close to our home. It was a ten-minute walk there along some nice meandering gravel trails. Then we went under the highway through the tunnel coming out at the creek with a small wading area that almost all the dogs love to soak in. It's a glorious place for the dogs. And oh, what a diverse human crowd it draws as well.

For me, I'm not sure what's more interesting though, the people or the dogs. It's amazing the differences and uniqueness in all the dogs; the sizes, the colours, coat markings and lengths, how they play and interact, it's just a real feast for the eyes and soul. You can also really see the personalities of the dogs come out. I love all this, but as I'm get older, what really makes me smile inside is I like listening to the banter by the owners and how they impart human voices, mannerisms, and characteristics to the dogs as they anthropomorphize their actions. I love to hear their personification banter of their dog! "Oh look at how the little shy puppy is playing with Maxie, he's saying come chase me or tug on the stick…". You've heard it, and most likely added to this banter yourself right! What a weird thing we do but it gets us humans talking and socializing.

Some give the play by play of what the dogs are doing just like a hockey announcer calling a game. Others "psychoanalyze" every dog's personality and predict their next interaction with the other dogs and why they are doing this or that! And all the while you and I stand there thinking, "Dang, what the heck is that person's name again?!" We all get to learn and know the dog's names but rarely do we get to know the person's name. This could be a person you see all the time and years can go by without us knowing! Funny enough though, the common bond of our dogs brings us together and a unique level of trust is shared. We tend to trust and open up with these people; we share about our kids, partners, personal issues, work challenges, health issues and so much more but we never ask their name! And when we finally do, we just as quickly forget it and end up back not knowing their name again. How embarrassing would it be if we have to ask for it again! Why does this happen to us?

We know the dogs need their exercise and socializing so we take them to the dog park. The dogs bring us together and it's this connection of trust as well as the sharing that is so important in the socializing. It makes us feel good, more relaxed, listened too and understood. This is the power of social connections. I'm so glad my dogs helped me with this.

It wasn't the first lesson I learned from my dogs, but as I'm getting older it's becoming more and more important and vital in my life. Having dogs and being exposed to the importance of the pack and socializing is one key lesson that has served me well. I look forward to developing and growing it more as I get older.

My simple insight that I learned from my dogs is don't be a loner, get in with the pack, socialize! Besides it's more fun with others. We are social beings and we need these interactions to be complete or whole. And now, current research is clearly showing social interactions make us happier and contribute to us living longer! Lift your spirits; go take your dog to the dog park and socialize!

And when you are there don't spent all your time on your phone, be present and really enjoy the quality time with them and the other **dog walkers**

LESSON 7
The Game of Catch

Understanding The Give And Take
I had just moved to Toronto from a small town called Lindsay. It was the end of August and it was my eighth birthday in 1968. We moved into a townhouse complex that would turn out to be a wonderful environment for kids to grow up in. The townhouse complex was surrounded by woods on two sides with a small meandering creek running through it. There were great tobogganing hills and big trees for rope swings, a labyrinth of an underground parking garage to play in, a paved walking path through the whole complex that acted as a race course for us kids on our bikes, there were lots of other kids and many dogs.

I had only seen this dog out being walked a few times and noticed the owners throwing the ball for him just the once. Yet, I walked over, knocked on their door and asked if I could throw the ball for the dog. "Sure I guess so" the owner stated. She gave me a few tennis balls and the dog came bounding out to play. He was a large golden retriever with long golden flowing hair, just like the hair I had at that time! And he knew the game.

The bright green tennis ball was covered in a white foamy, dog saliva goop! It had little splinters of grass, pine needles, small sticks and gravel all wrapped up with it. It looked gross and slimy. I didn't want to just grab it, as I knew this dog would then shift into a tug o' war mode with me and then I would have to fully grab the slime ball. And that was exactly what I didn't want to happen. Instead, I put my hands on either side of the great dogs mouth and he spit it out without any effort. He knew the game.

We didn't need to talk. No commands or sounds were shared. Just deep visceral communication from one simple eight year old creature to another. He wanted to run after the ball as he found it was fun and I wanted to throw the ball as I found it was fun. To be honest, I got a kick out of seeing him take off chasing the ball at full throttle. Running so fast and making these great athletic leaps to grab the ball then proudly trotting back to me with it.

There was a satisfying simple joy in seeing this guy run and catch that bouncing tennis ball. The higher I could throw it with the corresponding bigger bounces the better. There was a peaceful satisfaction playing catch. I wished I could run and jump like him! I'm sure he was smiling and I know he was happy. I sure was. What a great feeling this bond between dog and human. Giving and receiving. Throwing and catching (retrieving in this case). This was a win-win situation for both parties. He knew the game.

I was eight years old. I didn't know I was learning one of the key life lessons necessary to get ahead and thrive in the modern world. The skill of playing catch; throwing and catching. Giving and receiving. Ebbing and flowing. Giving to get. And a dog was the teacher!

Lack Or Abundance?

Lady and Casy where my role models for how dogs should act. Often I would go see my friend Mark who had a dog named Huxley. Huxley was a fun, kind and robust dog that spent too much time on a lead and not enough time running in the woods. He had a good nature about him however, he acted differently than my dogs. He would get overly protective of his sticks and downright nasty, showing his teeth if you came anywhere near him at meal time. I wasn't used to seeing this type of behaviour as my dogs seemed to get along and often ate from the same bowl. No big deal. To me, Huxley was out of balance. I think he saw the world through a lens of lack. Maybe he thought there was only so much food and this was his so he was going to protect it and keep it just for himself. I understood this as I too saw the world through the lens of lack. I was out of balance with this key equilibrium.

When I was living in Ghetto Village we had the usual stuff, a TV, table and chairs, cooking utensils and so on but we didn't have a lot. I often remember think, shish, I wish I had this or that. As a young man, this important equilibrium between giving and getting was way out of balance in my life. As I didn't have much in terms of physical things, I thought there wasn't much out there so I wanted to get more and I thought I had to hold on to it tight. It was all about me and what my needs were, what I needed to get. I had to get a job, I had to get a car, I had to get an apartment etc. I did the things I wanted to do when I wanted to do them. I didn't feel loved so I thought there was none in me to give. This mindset was very self-focused. It was all about me, me, me but it was also a symptom of something bigger going on. I had such a narrow and small view of the world that I believed the pie was limited and only so big, thus I wanted to get my piece of it one way or the other before the other guy did. I didn't know how to play the game yet.

In hindsight, I can now see how this out of balance equation limited and slowed my growth and development towards success in my life. My mindset was one of lack. I just wanted to get. There was little or no giving. If I was asked for a donation, there was no way I would give something, as I felt I didn't even have enough to survive. I thought I was the one that should have been getting a donation. To me, there was no extra to share, there was no abundance to share so my attitude was get what you can from the other guy and hold on to it tight. Lack was the lens through which I saw the world. Working and being with dogs at this point in my life helped enlighten this key understanding and rebalance the disharmony I was living.

I was becoming very fond of Lady and Casy and our bond was growing and getting deeper. I wanted something better for them. They were giving me a new perspective into life and the lessons I was learning were helping me dig myself out of the hellhole mess I was in. I was helping them learn new things and become well trained socialized dogs and in return I was getting some of that wonderful unconditional love. And I was learning to put others needs in front of my own. I was slowing learning the game. I was giving to get.

The thought was quite foreign to me at the time, I definitely didn't have this type of feeling or impulse often but I remember thinking how much I hated Ghetto Village and how I wanted something better for my two younger brothers and my mom whom I was living with. I knew this place was going to crush them the same way it was crushing me. I felt this incredible drive to somehow get us out of this place into a more supporting and conducive environment. I was going to have to work harder than ever to make the extra money to get us out of there. I wasn't going to do it for me; I was going to do it for them and the dogs.

Work, work, work. It took over three years of working 60, 70 and 80 hour weeks to save enough money to pay for my first year of university. I was twenty-four, just finishing high school and would be heading off to university. But there was a gut-wrenching problem. When I left I would be forever gone from Ghetto Village, but the others would be left behind continuing to be crushed by living in that dump. I couldn't swallow that pill. I just couldn't come to grips with leaving them there. My guts churned with the decision but my heart felt like it was singing. This would be the first big mature thing I had ever done. I put their needs ahead of mine. I took my tuition money and rented a townhouse for us far away from this place in a new and up and coming area called Scarborough. I would worry about how to pay for university later.

We got out of the jaws of that hellhole just in time. I was learning the game the dogs were teaching me, give to get, throw and catch. I was shifting my mindset from me to we, and my thinking from lack to abundance. This lesson was to serve me well many times in my later life.

In the late 1990's when our first daughter Jenna was born a new and strange thing started happening at parties and gatherings. I wasn't being called by my name. I was now referred to as "Jenna's Dad". The focus was shifting away from me to her. At work, the same thing would happen, I became "Robert from the company I worked for" or "The guy from X company is here". I was losing my identity and being put on the back burner, and it was bugging me. My ego really didn't like what was going on. I wanted the focus to be on me, I wanted the attention but it was our daughter's turn now. I think this was the mindset of lack in play. Lucky me, I got to learn and grow some more.

Maybe you've been in or are in a relationship where it feels like only one person is giving. You keep giving, they keep taking and it gets awkward. The throw and catch game isn't being played in the equal balance anymore. Resentment and bitterness can develop. You may even think that if they aren't giving then I'm not going to give and start holding back your love and caring. You know how this ends, the relationship heads to the finish line. You become roommates with no intimacy or connection. No one is giving and no one is getting. The mindset of lack rules! The game isn't being played.

In business relationships this dance can get out of balance and unfold the same way. One company maybe giving a huge amount of resources to another expecting something of value in return and nothing of reciprocating value is returned. There may be activity but nothing of true value is returned. One gives, one takes but there is no return. There is no synergy, no give and take, no throw and catch. The game stops. The mindset of lack rules! Their mindset of what's in it for me, what can I get from them, this attitude of me verses we is in play. They see the world through the lens of lack. They won't get ahead and be successful thinking and being like that.

What would happen if you went to the park with your dog and just threw the ball without them retrieving it? How much fun would that be just throwing the ball, getting it yourself and then throwing it again! How longing would you keep that up? The dog may be amused but you wouldn't be. I know it might be highly simplified but I think you will get the point, there has to be a give and take. You need a throw and a return for it to be fun. And when the dog does their part and retrieves the ball, what a hoot! But it can get even better if you make the game more interesting and challenging!

Old Dog - New Tricks
What if you hide the ball and have the dog then sniff it out to retrieve it. Or what if you put three different objects out and teach them the difference between them, then give the command for them to get the one you ask for, and they do it correctly! How amazing is that? What about if you hide and they have to seek you out by using their other senses? Oh what fun and oh how rewarding. Turning work into play, learning and growing, throwing and catching is what it's all about. I like the word synergize. It's more that just win-win, it's where each party gets more than they invested and are really happy with the return. As I also discovered, this also works great with kids!

I was in my late forties when it started to dawn upon me that my challenges and hurdles early in my life were great resources for understanding what others wanted to discover. Being able to reflect and recognize new insights from my past with the dogs has been a source of gold. Learning how to turn my troubles into treasures has been a huge blessing and mental relief. And it's very rewarding helping others.

When I started to realize that I actually had something of value to give to the world and that people wanted to hear what I had to say it hit me, there's more than enough to go around. There's incredible abundance, so give some of it away. Share the goodness. It helps others and I get to feel great. And this ties into the idea of living a life that matters, a life with significance, a life with meaning and purpose that's rewarding and fulfilling.

As I've gone through life and spent many years training and helping others get what they want I can now understand the importance of "we" over "me". Honestly, the pie really is way bigger than one can imagine. There is an abundance of success to be had as well. There's lots and lots to go around for everyone. There is no lack. My mindset is now that of abundance, of sharing and giving back to those who are open to learning and growing. It really is about others and our relationships.

It's about synergizing and doing more with more so we all win bigger. It's deeply fulfilling being able to contribute to others growth and development and seeing them get their wings and fly. It's about doing the dance of giving and taking, throwing and catching, giving to get. A fundamental lesson of getting along in the world that dogs helped instill in me.

Understanding and applying the game of throw and catch and shifting my mindset from lack to abundance to my own life has allowed me to help my family in the ways I could and then on a larger scale it's allowed me to contribute more to my working and business community. This has made the struggle all worth it.

I often think about that big golden retriever and throwing the ball for him. What a simple but vital lesson, the game of catch, he taught me and how important that has been in my life. I reflect and think about Lady and Casy and the great joy, pride and fulfillment they gave me as I learned how to shift my mindset from me to we and how I was able to help so many other improve their lives with that lesson. And I think about Max and how much he gave to my family and me. There was an abundance of love and caring in him for all. He taught us to see the world through the lens of abundance.

LESSON 8
Presence

It could be raining or sunny, it didn't matter, any little sound of a branch swishing, a stick breaking, other dogs barking or a bird calling, Lady and Casy were in tune to the environment. Noses to the ground or high in the air smelling the smallest of scents, they were present and highly focused in the moment. All their senses were on full operational alert. They were right there, in that very moment. I'm sure they weren't thinking about yesterday, this morning, my rants or what was for dinner tonight. Their whole sensory system was attuned to the current moment, the here and now. And when we were engaged playing tug o' war with a stick or playing fetch with a ball, the same thing was occurring. They were focused on the moment and me. They were truly present.

What a blessing to be privy to such focus. What an incredible lesson to be learned and shared, the ability to be present. This lesson of focusing and getting present to the moment right now is another one of those wonderful lessons I've learned from the dogs in my life. It has helped me in my relationships, business interactions and in sports. I've also noticed that the ability to be and stay present in our modern society is waning. This can't be good for our relationships.

It had been one of those long draining days. I had been working at a convention that started at seven AM. I was up and out of the house just before six. The drive home through the Toronto airport traffic was brutally slow. It was now after seven. My stomach was calling. I was zonked mentally and physically and needed to get some stuff of my chest and vent about the day. I was sharing how my day went and how I was feeling. I was just looking for some comfort and support. Some emotional bonding if you will. It wasn't happening. I was getting more irritated and frustrated with their actions. It was really pissing me off. I needed some emotional closeness and they weren't present to me! That damn texting is so distracting! ARG!

I have a short attention span and get distracted very easily, too easily my wife often reminds me. It's tough work and takes a lot of effort for me to stay in the moment, on task and to be present. And if someone I'm speaking to finds their phone more interesting, or if they can't resist checking it for some "important" message, I'm gone. The connection breaks and my brain takes me to another place. If I'm trying to connect with someone and they disengage by being on their phone it sends me the signal that the phone is more important than the person in front of them, me! I think we all sense this unfitting behaviour but it's becoming the social norm. When the abnormal becomes the normal we have a problem! I wonder what kind of social issues this is going to create. It takes two to tango as the old saying goes and I'm looking for people to dance with.

In your own life have you noticed that many are physically present but mentally distant? Their body is here but their mind is far away somewhere else in a virtual world. They leave your surroundings and get teleported to someplace else through their phone or device. I think we all know that you can't mentally be in two places at once. It sends me the signal that they aren't interested in me and that the other virtual world is more important. They're disengaged and I get ready to leave.

But I'm no angel. Be honest and tell me if you've done this before. You've been on your phone, highly engaged in something and you trip over a little stone or your own feet, or a curb, or even bump into other people because you were more focused on your phone than your surroundings. Talk about absent-minded! Let's be realistic, we are all guilty of doing this at some time. There have been incidents of people walking into a vehicle and being killed because they were on their phone and distracted. Sadly, they were definitely not present in the moment.

I've heard the argument that our devices allow us to be more connected to family and friends. I think this is true, we are more connected however, I've observed and felt that the technology is also keeping others at an emotional distance. A book entitled "Alone Together" by MIT professor Shirley Turkle shares some interesting insights on this. She shared that many are looking for technology to bring them closer together in relationships but at the same time they use the technology to protect themselves from the relationship; read this as getting too close and being hurt. We're lonely but fear intimacy and being hurt.

Some use texting so they don't have to reveal too much about themselves. And it doesn't take much time! It gives the illusion of companionship without the demands of friendship. "Texting offers just the right amount of access, just the right amount of control…texting puts people not too close, not too far, but at the just the right distance." The goldilocks effect if you will. (As a side note, I wonder if this is why so many are getting dogs. They fear intimacy and the potential hurt of lost love but want the company and love that dogs provide without the commitment?

When I was younger love used to be spelled T.I.M.E. Time was necessary to cultivate a relationship. You had to invest time in the other person to build the bond. I sometimes wonder if the virtual world is stunting our ability to be close in the physical world. I've recently read that the best way to improve your sex life is to not take your phone to bed! Really! Hello! Do we actually need some guru to tell us this? I guess common sense isn't always common practice!

Living and working with dogs has taught me to live more in the now, to be more present and to fully appreciate the awe of now. I have also found that being present also reduces the regret of wasting or squandering ones time. I love the equation that time equals life. Wasting our time is equal to wasting our life. Value our time, spend it wisely living by our true values, being present and we have a life of fulfillment, satisfaction and peace of mind. How good is that!

We all have phones and other screens that we can be on and often we are on them way too much. They seem to have taken over our life as our life now evolves around our phone! Yes social media is good but you know what I think is better? I think it's real life with those who are right here with you. Right here, right now! So many are living through their phones that they're missing the real show, the real authentic experience of life, which is the present moment.

Think about this, we're using TV, iPads and other devices to distract our children to stop them from interfering with "our time", which selfishly is our time with our devices. I want my kids to be better off than I was. Interestingly, I feel like I have to give them more than what I had growing up including more presents. And now, funny enough, they seem to have too much stuff, too many distractions and are in turn being pulled in too many directions so their attention span is measured in nano seconds. I'm always struggling with this conflict; do they really need more stuff and more presents or do they essentially need me to be more present for them! Do they simply need my presence?

Eckhart Tolle wrote a book called The Power of Now. Not the Power of Tomorrow or The Power of Yesterday. It is called The Power of NOW. Being in the moment and really present, and connected! This is what dogs do. Dogs always seem present and connected to you, and this is something I think we can all learn from. And maybe this is why they're always happy. I've snuck up on my dogs many times when they were busy and focused on chewing a stick, or chewing a ball and startled them. It made me laugh! They were so in the moment and present to chewing that they didn't even hear me coming up to them, even with their incredible hearing they had turned all their attention to the chewing. By the way, Eckhart Tolle is a dog guy.

This ability to focus and be present is a huge asset and advantage in business as well as in life situations. Drifting in and out of conversations makes for poor communications, sending mixed messages and reduces productivity. Watch out for people who say they can multitask. Don't be fooled by this idea that you're getting more done multitasking. That's been proven not to be true. The good advice is to be truly present and focus on the task or communication at hand, finish up, then move on. A sad and preventable state is that of using devices when driving. This is now almost as big a killer as drinking and driving. What is that telling us about our presence?

I was reading a study that spoke about how now so many people in today's busy society don't feel listened to and even sadder, very few actually felt understood.

A deep belief I have is that the biggest gift we can give our children is our presence so we can understand them and they can understand us. They don't need more stuff, more presents, they need us to be there, listening to them and communicating at a deeper level. None of this "Hmm, yes dear" stuff. I think this applies to our other relationships as well. We need to be truly here and present. My dogs have had to teach me this lesson more than a few times. I'm a slow learner! But I'm getting it, the importance of being present.

Get More From The Moment

Winter hadn't let go yet and spring was just budding. The ground was a mess. The sidewalks were loaded with sand and salt from the winter. The trails were a goopy, slimy, muddy mess. I remember walking Max through the slush and mud. It was such a mess. He was a mess! And I had work to do, chores to finish up and stuff to do. I just wanted to get this walk over. I just wanted to get through it. Interesting enough though, Max had a very different attitude than mine!

All these new smells must have been awaking from the ground. New life was emerging. There were so many new things that were all around he couldn't get enough of them but I couldn't appreciate or value them. I was just trying to get through the walk. His paws, legs and underside were covered in mud. I was going to have to spray him down again when we got home. ARG! More stuff to do! I was living in the future, fretting over the stuff I had to do.

In the distance we saw one of his dog friends. As we approached they ran to each other and they started to play. Both dogs were still young and so full of energy and athleticism. It was a marvel to watch them run, play fight, and chase. I kept yelling, "Come on, lets go". Then it hit me. I was missing so much because I was living in the future. I wasn't present to the now. I wasn't appreciating what was right in front of me. I wasn't taking from the day; rather I was just trying to get through it.

This hasn't just happened with my dogs. This has happened with my children and even times with my wife. Can you relate? I've tried to push back and fight against this, to be more present and cognizant with my own children. I've tried to minimize the many distractions, and delights in my life, to be there for them. I put the last sculpture I was working on and started in 1997 on hold as my wife was pregnant and had just given birth to our first child who is now twenty-one! Indeed the clock spins fast. Time goes by and we can't even remember events or special moments because we're living in the future. (I could say, thank goodness for our phone camera. We will at least have pictures to cue our memory.)

Do you want to remember that special moment with your lover? Do you want to remember that unique experience during your holiday? It's easy; just get present and slow time. We can get so caught up in the moment, so focused that time seems to stand still. We check the clock and a huge chunk of time went by and we didn't even notice it. We can slow time. We can draw out every precious second of the moment when we are really there. And actually really present! Stay young at heart and don't grow up too fast. And let's not make our kids do this either. We may have blown it for ourselves, so lets teach them some new, more supporting ways of being. Lets teach them to be present. A great way to do this is by leading by example.

How To Get Present

Give people especially those close to you your complete uninterrupted attention. Don't just give them your physical closeness; give them your complete attention. As a challenge don't leave them for Google or Facebook or a text. Give them your mental, emotional, spiritual and physical attention. What a great way to build closeness. Get more engaged in the conversation. Get curious about their opinions and views and how and why they feel a particular way. This shows your presence and that you care! They will really appreciate this.

I was listening to an interview by Martha Beck speaking about one of her many books called *finding your own North Star*. She brought up the term "wordlessness". That is when our verbal brain becomes quiet and other areas of the brain open up to a new vast intelligence, which then allows us to get in tune with our instincts. This is when we get really present. To get there we have to stop thinking in language and let this other area of the brain go to work coming up with solutions to problems or coming up with new ideas.

Maybe you have experienced this diving your car. You're driving along and then some wonderful thought or idea pops into you mind. What's going on here? The left side of your brain is very busy processing the road conditions, traffic, surroundings etc. thus in turn freeing up the right side of your brain, the creative side, to work on problems and come up with those creative solutions, or new insights. You can get all these wonderful thoughts, you solve many of your own problems, or you may get that fantastic new idea.

This concept of becoming wordlessness to get in touch with your instincts can go to an even deeper level where you become truly present and connect into your instincts. We have all seen athletes make the sport they're doing look so easy and effortless. We think to ourselves, "That looks easy, I could do that". This highly focused and present state is described as flow. It's as if the brain isn't thinking and the body is just moving effortlessly by itself. This is when one has tapped into one's instincts. This is when one is most present and often feels the most alive. We come alive in the moment. This is when our worries, problems and concerns are gone. Martha Beck suggested that moving through nature in some way enhances this experience.

This holds true for me as well. I have found a few ways to get really present in my life. These include exercising in the woods, (running, mountain bike riding, skiing), riding my dirt bikes or when I'm intimate with my wife. Interesting enough, when I'm in that state

I also feel the most alive. As you can imagine, everyone needs to find his or her own way to get there.

I've found that when I'm out in nature doing something physical my verbal mind becomes quiet and my deeper inner voice percolates through. Sometimes when this happens I'm walking in the woods with the dogs. I get so many ideas, my troubles disappear and life is good! Martha Beck also suggested using a mantra when you are walking helps to allow the verbal mind to quiet so you can get to this state faster.

And finally, she also stated that moving through nature at the edge of your ability is a good way to quiet the verbal mind. She enjoyed downhill skiing. I've found riding dirt bikes, mountain bikes or playing hockey gets me there. Interestingly enough, every single person who I've ever mentioned this to agrees, when you are riding dirt bikes you are fully present. There is no other way; you snooze, you loose (crash). I think that's part of the addiction and love for bikes, riding them makes us so present to the moment that it makes us feel so alive and appreciative of life. You don't have to ride dirt bikes, you can you get "caught up" in whatever task you really enjoy and focus on it. This will produce the same end result, presence!

I used to love running with my dogs in the deeps woods in the summer. Looking over and seeing them do what mother nature designed them to do; run with their nose to the ground, finding new scents, tracking, jumping, and effortlessly maneuvering though the woods is incredible to watch. It was so amazing when they looked to me for cues and guidance, as I was the alpha in our pack. What was super cool was just using hand signals to communicate as we ran and then seeing them respond to the signals and carry out the request. What a truly amazing bond it is between dogs and humans. It was so primal. I felt so alive and honoured to be present to the moment with them.

I'm not perfect, I make mistakes and screw up all the time. But I'm getting better. I'm working and practicing at being more present. I turn my phone off more, I don't read or be distracted when at a table with others, I listen more intently and reflect back to people when they are speaking to show I'm listening and tuned in. I ask more questions to clarify things I don't understand. I want to build closer relationships and understand others. I want to be more present.

I think we know this stuff but we might not always do it. I want to become more mindful of the distractions in my life, cut them out and see how my relationships and business interactions are enhanced. Follow the example that dogs can give us. Be present in the now.

Slow time and get more out of the moment and life! I know it will make us happier.

LESSON 9
Happiness

My late teens and early twenties were very volatile and unstable. My temper was quite hot-blooded and I was known to have rants or should I say rages. I was still frustrated, angry and pissed at people and the world. My life direction and circumstances hadn't yet shifted to where I wanted it to be. Living in Ghetto Village was still just as crappy as always. Lucky enough for me though, because of my new bond with these dogs, Lady and Casy, something inside of me was changing or awakening. I seemed to have a broader range of emotions. Watching them run, play, and work I noticed that they were always happy and this filled me with joy and intrigue. It made me feel the same way I wished and wanted my life to be- happy.

And here is the real surprising part that blew me away about their way of being; my crappy attitude, yelling and scolding didn't seem to bother them. The dogs didn't seem to care about yesterday when I was yelling at them, being harsh or when I was in a pissy mood. They didn't hold a grudge or resentment towards me. They just let it go. They didn't think about tomorrow or next week and the 70 hours they would have to work. No, they were present today, right here, right now, in the moment at hand. And, they were happy. It wasn't just one magical thing that seemed to make dogs happy, it's was the combination of how they lived. It was their sunny attitude. They always seemed happy and grateful for the day and me.

Letting Go Of Yesterday
The thought slowly dawned on me, maybe if I want to be happier I should learn to let things go? Maybe I should try to enjoy

the day more. Maybe I should re-evaluate things from my past and draw new conclusions about them. Maybe I could find new meanings that would serve and support me in more positive ways. And maybe this was a way to reduce my bitterness and anger at the world. I wondered, what can I be thankful and appreciative of in my life today? This may sound nice, but it took years for me to see and feel the changes where I could say that I was actually happy. I had my moments but they were fleeting. My fab fifties were still a long way away.

I had just turned 50 when we first got Max in late 2010. He was still a puppy and like any dog, he sometimes had "accidents" in the house. I understood and respected this and we did our best to make sure he was frequently taken out. He learned quickly to hold it until we got him outside. As you now know Max was our first family dog that we chose with the kids. He was part mini poodle and part Golden-doodle. He was a smart fellow and he had quite an incredible memory.

He could find balls I hid a week earlier or sticks he had left on the trail last week. He had no problems remembering those other dog walkers, the ones with the liver treats that he had only met once before. He could remember the difference between sticks, balls, and Frisbees. So I know his memory worked well.

So the few times when we came home after leaving Max alone and there was a rather nicely sized turd with all it's wafting "aroma" in the boarded off sections of the living room, the room with the nice handmade wool carpet, I would lose it. Why the hell did he jump in there to do his business? He could have simply done it on his area on the papers or on the ceramic floor. He knew better. I wasn't a good model father for the kids at these times as I yelled and scolded him.

I knew he had a good memory. Thus it wasn't him forgetting about the times I was upset or yelled at or scolded him. Rather it seemed it was his conscious choosing to let these times go and move on. Yesterday wasn't that important anymore. He was letting the past go, forgiving, forgetting and moving on with our relationship. I'm sure he had a choice. He could have chosen to be grumpy, resentful or bitter but he didn't. He chose to be happy.

I also observed this trait in the other dogs in my life. It was great lesson to understand. Dogs let it go to be happy. They forget about yesterday and start today fresh with a clean slate and a positive upbeat curiosity. They don't carry judgments, hurts and emotions from yesterday into today. They seem to know instinctually how to be happy and letting stuff go is part of that process. Indeed, they seem really good at letting things go and moving on with the relationship.

Have you noticed that this isn't always the case with us humans though. Many seem to hold on to yesterday with resentment and bitterness, even stewing in it. Letting it go is an important lesson I wanted to master. It has served me well many times and it was key to me being happier with my life. I needed to let go of my negative past and negative thinking to make way for the positive happier future I wanted.

What I noticed in my dogs is that the ability to let things go seems to be one important key for their happiness. Dogs don't judge us on our size, colour, or shape, just our actions and behaviours, and sometimes our smell. They see our real character through our faults and accept us for who we are. They see through our "human image", the one we try to impress other humans with. Our real character is revealed to them by our actions and behaviour, not by superficial traits. They don't care about our designer clothes or fancy cars. This is part of the unconditional love and deep loyalty they have to us, their owners and caregivers.

They don't hold grudges. They are able to let yesterday go. They forgive and forget and simply move on to the present, the here and now. They don't hold a grudge and hate you if you opened the door and banged them by accident when you came in the front door or stepped on their foot as you got up from the dinner table. They let all that stuff go, so they can be happier.

Don't Get Down To Be Happy

It's actually a simple thing not to do to be happier. Don't get down on yourself. Dogs don't get down on themselves. They don't have the same self-inflicted mental pains, worries or anxieties we have. Think about it. Why do you think they call them "therapy dogs"? They are "treatment" for many of our modern ailments. People find them calming and relaxing. Patting them can stir fond memories of their history with a dog back in the day. Their blood pressure comes down; they smile and laugh as their spirits are lifted. That's the "healing" power of having a dog in your presence.

Compare this to the self-inflicted poisons we induce upon ourselves. Many are full of toxic resentment, bitterness, and anger. We hold grudges, we judge, and label others in negative ways. We are always wanting, never having enough and we don't seem to be content with what we have and who we are. We hold onto the past with regret and can't make room for the future to come into our lives.

And to make matters worse, we are so hard on ourselves. We keep comparing ourselves to the perfect people on TV and idealist Facebook posts of others who seem to have perfect lives. We can't keep up with the huge quantity of how to be great at something books or videos. We self impose incredible standards and raise the bar so high, we can never hit it leading to defeat, lack of enthusiasm and energy and an empty soul. We then starting thinking we're not good enough. What a terrible non-supporting mindset to have that rids one of happiness.

Dogs don't ever seem to worry about how good they are or if they are worthy of your love and affection. Sure, they want us to like them and for us to be the alpha, but I'm sure they don't fret over their "worthiness". They aren't overly concerned with their height, fur colour, colour of their eyes, how big their ears, paws or bellies are, or if they pass gas.

Dogs aren't programed with societal beliefs. They don't know if they're a poodle, golden retriever, shih tzu, bulldog or greyhound. They don't want all kinds of things and thus they aren't depressed and let down when they don't get them. They aren't trying to keep up with the "Jones" or others. They don't seem to have the baggage of preconceived notions or expectations we have. They are always open and curious to the day, the surroundings and life! They take as much as they can from the day instead of just getting through it. Having a positive mindset and attitude is such an important lesson that that my dogs taught me to be happy.

How can we discover what our mindset is about health as an example? I've heard it put as the "naked truth". Strip down naked and take a deep long look into the mirror. What you will see staring back is the outside reflection of what's going on inside your head (your belief about health). As I discovered, it was my (poor) mindset, philosophy and attitude that was the driving force behind my state in life. They impacted the choices I made, the actions I took or didn't take, which gave me the results I had in my life. It was that simple.

As I began to understand in life, one's mindset and attitude are everything. It has been interesting to observe over the last 30 years of working and teaching about nutrition, that almost 100% of the people that go on a diet to lose weight gain it back. They think the weight is the problem and thus if they lose it, life will be rosy and the problem will be gone. Many, including myself, never understood that the weight wasn't the problem. It was my mindset, my attitude and my philosophy that was the problem. The weight (or in my case, the trouble) was just a "symptom", an outcome of my philosophy. I love the quote by Darren Hardy; "You will only have the level of health that matches your level of self" (yourself image and self-worth). When you look in the mirror it's not to see your body, rather it's to see the results of your mindset, attitude and philosophy on your health. This applies to our happiness as well.

And here is more amazing news, we can take back control and boost our happiness. The solution is to go to work on us. Not our weight, relationships or finances but ourselves. Work on who we are, our beliefs about our personal philosophy, and who we want to become. Write down some of your key values and start living by them on a daily basis. We can never become closer to our real self and be truly authentic and happy unless we stop justifying, complaining and blaming others for our problems and issues. We have to step up and take full responsibility for our mindset, actions and results. Then we're being true to ourselves and living a more authentic life. Envision the updated 2.0 you and go about making it happen. Think about how lucky we are, that we can choose how our days are going to be and how we want our life to unfold. How wonderful is that. This is an effective technique for boosting happiness.

Wants vs. Needs For Happiness

I can be a sucker for infomercials. I've always been this way. I know it and I try to fight it. Even today as I approach sixty I sill get pulled in. There is an incredible life lesson for me here and maybe you can relate. Even though I know about the effects of it, I have been known to get caught up in marketing and advertising for products. It could be the latest greatest tool, TV, electronic device, car or what not, but I get drawn in, hook, line and sinker as they say.

And why was I getting caught up in this dance? Because like many I believed that if I had that thing(s) I would be happier. Having it would *make me* happier! This was the power of extrinsic factors on my ego. I thought I needed extrinsic (or outside) factors to make me happy. Many times I would work and save for something I thought I really wanted and then almost as soon as I got it, the desire for it and the happiness I thought it would give me was gone in a fleeting moment. And what happened next? You guessed it. I replaced it with a new want, a new desire and the cycle continued. Drawing upon the importance of being more true and authentic to ourselves, if you don't know what it is that makes you happy, material items may only give you short-term happiness.

As I learned from my dogs, happiness comes from within, not from outside external things- the extrinsic factors. As I've worked and lived with dogs it has become clear to me I've had to break the mindset and stop thinking happiness came from the outside. I now understand that it's something we generate from the inside. I had to choose to be happy and then happily achieve as I move through the day. As I explored this concept more I started asking if my things were making me happy? Yes? No? Maybe? And would more stuff make me even happier? There is now much written about why it may be better to invest in experiences verses more stuff. We explored some of this when I spoke about the lesson of simplification I learned from my dogs.

A few times in this book I talk about how "constructed consumerism" is driving the market place and generating all kinds of desires and "wants" in us and how we "think" we need these things to be happy. Please understand, these are subconscious desires and may not be the true solutions to make you happy. Maybe we aren't thinking on our own and using our own good judgment. Could it be that the map or compass we use to find happiness and the cues that signal happiness are wrong!

I know as humans we have greater needs and wants than dogs. I understand and get it. We all want to fulfill Maslow's hierarchy and achieve self-actualization, but what price do we pay? And do we pay the right price? For example, working 50 or 60+ hours per week, or self-isolation due to excess device usage, or little or no association with nature and our surroundings? I can't tell you how to live, but I hope I can generate thoughts and questions you can ask yourself to make sure you are paying the "right" price for the life you want.

In his bestselling book on success Stephen Covey clearly stated, "Most people spend their whole lives climbing the ladder of success only to realize when they get to the top, the ladder has been leaning against the wrong wall!" How terrible one must feel if that happens. It has been noted that many close to their last day on earth will talk not about all the great stuff they had or the things they did, rather they bemoan the regrets they have for the things they should have or could have done! What can we learn from them?

Reflecting back on the almost 60 years of my life, I now understand the equation that time equals life. Wasting our time equals wasting our life. Valuing our time equals a life of fulfillment, satisfaction and peace of mind. We need to know what our truest, deepest values are and live by them. This will get us closer to our real happiness. Being more present in the moment and the day is another. Live life awake. Happy days equate to a happy life.

As I slowly ponder over the latest flyers or magazines that came to our door I'm often flooded with the thought that a particular item would be nice to have. But then I have to ask myself, is this something I really need or is this something I really want? If I feel like I really want it why do I want it? What "need" will it fill? How will it make me feel owning this item? What is the need behind the need? My wife is very good at helping me with this. This self-inquiry helps me surface and identify some of my driving behaviours and allows me a deeper insight into myself thus allowing me to be more true and authentic to me. This also helps put me on the road to greater happiness.

What Makes You Happy?

It's pretty clear what makes a dog happy; food, friends, being near you, their owner and sleeping. So here is another nudge for you, what makes you happy? Do you know? Interestingly, most don't. In the book *Stumbling on Happiness*, Professor Dan Gilbert wrote about how most don't know what makes them happy. And those that thought they knew were wrong! How could this be? If it isn't the money, the clothes or the cars that actually make us happy then what does? As stated earlier, it could be that we have and are following the wrong maps to happiness. Maybe the mental guidelines and cues we're following to achieve happiness are outdated and wrong!

You know how optical illusions can fool our eyes? Dan Gilbert makes the argument that our brains systematically misjudge what will make us happy. The assumptions that we make about what will make us happy are often wrong. And these quirks in our cognition are what make humans very poor predictors of our own bliss! We blindly end up chasing something that won't make us happy once we get it. We're told to follow *our bliss* to happiness, not follow *someone else's* bliss!

Have you heard the idea that happiness is the reward of hard work? The idea is that when we're successful we'll be happy, but this idea maybe wrong. Research is showing that it's the people who go about their day happy who are the most successful. Have you heard this or stated this to yourself sometime; "I'll be happy when X happens", or "When I do or have X, I'll be happy then", or "Once I achieve X, I'll be happy". What do these statements tell us? They seem to imply that we can only be happy once we achieve or get something in the future. You may know this as the "I'll be happy when…"concept. Watch out for this. There is a problem with this mindset in that with each success the goal post of happiness gets pushed out further and farther preventing us from actually getting there. Just like the pot of gold at the end of a rainbow, we keep chasing it but we can never get it. The future "then" never happens and we end up living in a constant state of unhappiness. And with this, we don't feel fulfilled or satisfied and happiness eludes us. But we can change this.

We all need to wake up and knock this false belief of "I'll be happy when" concept out of our heads. It's screwing up so many people. If we slow down and look around at all the peoples of the world, we will clearly see what many innately know, but may have forgotten. It's that happiness is not something to be acquired in the future. It is something to be experienced now! You are either happy or... you're not! If you aren't happy now, you probably won't be in the future. The time to be happy is NOW! Eckhart Tolle wrote a book entitled *The Power of NOW*. Become present to the now. Be here NOW. Be happy NOW! It can't get any simpler. Just take a look at how your dog and the dogs in the dog park are. They live for now. They don't fret over the future thinking they'll be happy when they get something. They're happy now. Happiness is how you live. This is what I'm striving to do each day, I work on going about my day happily achieving my goals and making my dreams come alive.

New Maps To Happiness

What does it take for us to be happy? Happiness is an interesting emotion to achieve as it's based on our assumptions, beliefs, labels and the rules that we've accepted and incorporated into our subconscious that have to be met for us to feel and be happy. Some call these "mental maps". These give us the directions or are the formula that we need to be happy. The million-dollar question is "But what if you're not happy"? What is going on or not going on that is preventing us from experiencing this positive emotion?

Something to consider is, are the criteria or directions to happiness right for you? Are your mental maps non-supporting and misdirecting you? And, digging a little deeper, are the criteria and directions to happiness actually yours or are they instilled from society, family or other peers? I have to ask, are we following and living other's mental maps? And could this be one reason we aren't as blissful as we wish?

The same way we can update the maps in a GPS unit in our car, maybe we need to update our mental maps so it's easier for us to hit our destination of happiness and experience this positive emotion. Maybe we need to reevaluate the rules and parameters that determine if we're happy or not.

Alan Watts stated, "You are under no obligation to be the same person you were five minutes ago." As well, you are under no obligation to settle or keep your current lifestyle and situation. It's in your power to change it. For some, boosting happiness may come down to regaining control and changing their life. This is easy once you accept that fact that you can control your life by exercising your "choosing muscle". This is intentional living where one lives on purpose.

I'm not sure if it was relief or liberation that I felt, but when I had the realization that I don't have to change, but rather, I could choose to change and grow, a new sense of happiness came over me. This control was empowering. I could choose who and what I wanted to be. I could plan out my direction in life and take action to make it happen. It was exciting.

Give Yourself Credit

There seems to be another quirky thing humans do to prevent us from being happier we under value our hard work and achievements. According to Nobel Prize winning professor Daniel Kahneman, we are hardwired to undervalue a gain and over value a loss. He summarizes it as "The aggravation and negative emotions we experience associated to a loss appear to be greater than the pleasure and positive emotions associated with gaining something of equal value."

How does this impact our daily living? For one thing we undervalue our positive actions and don't give ourselves due credit when we do something good, great or positive. And here is the part that gets us down, we over value our actions when we do something wrong, negative or inappropriate. Basically, we blow things out of proportion. We get down on ourselves. This inhibits our forward progression and doesn't let us build up any momentum. We fill our brains with negative self-talk which is non-supporting.

What can we learn from the professionals to reduce this impact of under valuing a gain and over valuing a loss? Let's look at professional sports teams as an example. Every time they score a goal, basket or touchdown they celebrate. Notice what else they do. They will also celebrate every small step on the way there. The last play, the good catch or pass. They look for the good in a situation and celebrate the progress. And what happens if something happens to turn things around in a negative way, what do they then do? They tell themselves it could have been worse. We'll get it back, we'll turn things around, and let's get back on top.

I didn't know it at the time but this is what I was doing when I was living in Ghetto Village. With all the associated challenges and issues going on in my life I was overwhelmed to the point of being stifled. I couldn't make any moves to get ahead until the ways of being I was learning from the dogs started impacting me. As my mindset and attitude starting shifting I was able to take tiny little steps that slowly helped nudge me forward ever so slightly. I never saw these actions as "wins". They were simply matter of fact things that just had to be done.

I started building a ladder of hope. I took control of the very few things I could control and I acted upon them. No big fancy plan for me. I just started taking action, just simple little steps on the things I could control. This was expanding my options; this gave me hope and more control. There was so much I didn't know so I only acted on the things I did know. I was redefining my mental maps and charting a new course for my life.

Just like the professional sport teams, this is what I was doing. I learned that I felt better when I would celebrate all the tiny little milestones. And I do mean every little thing. From getting up and making it to work, to eating better food for dinner, to reading ten pages of a book, everything was fuel for me. It was important for me to celebrate all wins and positives however small they were. I wanted Lady and Casy to behave better as well so I used this "strategy" on them. Every time they did something we liked, we praised them and give them a good pat or rub and maybe even a treat. They loved it and tended to want to keep doing the behaviour to get our praise. You see, in many ways we are just like dogs! Positive praise does wonders for us as well.

Again, I want to help nudge you forward, so I would ask, what can you do in your life right now to celebrate your wins to reinforce the positives? I have a bias towards physical actions as the movement helps generates positive brain chemicals and emotions (motion generates emotion). It can be as easy as a high five with someone, a fist pump as you yell "YES" (visualize the tennis player when they make that amazing winning point), a firm pat on the back of colleague -if appropriate for the office setting- as you tell them way to go, good job etc. You could even do a "happy dance". It could be a dinner out, a small gift to yourself etc. It doesn't matter what it is, it's the fact of doing it that matters.

Doing this on a consistent basis will build up our confidence, self-esteem and just make us feel better. We will start building our ability to take action and move ahead with projects, tasks and goals in our life. We start getting more "juiced" over the future and start looking forward to it verses dreading it! We start looking for the good. It helps lift our mood, and it builds more positive associations to tasks. It can also keep us rolling as it builds our momentum and that makes that next big thing much easier to tackle and move towards. And further, we get more done and we enjoy our day more. And for our friends and family, we're a lot more fun to be around when we are happy.

People Pleasers

The greeting from my dogs was a highlight of my day. It always lifted my spirit and made me feel loved, appreciated and needed. It didn't matter want kind of day I was having, coming home to one or a few dogs it didn't matter, there was always much enthusasm and joy, all for seeing me! Afterwards, the dogs would come and lay down near me when I was at home. It was such a wonderful feeling knowing they wanted to be close to me. I'm sure your dog(s) do this as well. (And yes, cats may even do this.) But has your dog ever come over and tried to make you happy? They may want to play, but this is for their satisfaction not yours. Yet strange enough, many of us humans go though our day or life trying to make others happy.

It has been well documented that many people are either trying to make others happy such as parents, family, boss etc. or they are chasing the definition or idea of happiness imposed by society, the media, culture, and TV. What's devious about this though, it may be subconscious. Thus we need to make this a conscious choice to define what it is that makes up happy! So I ask you, whose idea of success are you living out? What is your definition of happiness? My advice is to be authentic. Be you. Dogs aren't caught up in their image impressing others with things and wealth, unless they have just found and have a nice big stick to chew. And even then, they look for another dog to play tug with them.

Quiet the voice that tells us what to do, the reason we should do things voice, the voice to be practical, conservative, safe, responsible. This is the voice of obligation and guilt. Following that voice may lead you down an unhealthy path. My advice would be to question it. Never stop asking, am I following my heart? Am I doing the things that give me the greatest pleasure and meaning in my life? Are the things I'm doing actually making me happy? Hear the inner voice that calls us.

Find your inner compass. Tap into your inner source of guidance. I love watching the dogs run through the woods, nose to the ground using their instincts, being who they genetically are. They are truly awake and truly living authentically in the moment. And they are so happy! What can we learn from them?

You may need a quiet reflective time to calm and quiet the voice in your brain and allow your inner voice to come through. You can stop the verbal chatter of the mind and get in touch with your "belly brain" and instincts by moving through nature to put the verbal brain to sleep. This allows the right side of the brain to work on solutions to the challenges you may have and to surface your inner voice. Listen to that inner voice to find out what makes you happy. Then, follow and do the things that make you happy so your soul can sing.

Compare Or Contrast

Here is something more to ponder, what actually is happiness? Some will say it's an illusion. We make up an idea in our heads as to what it is. And, we only know if we are happy by taking our idea and comparing it to something else. Often we compare it to other people. This goes back to the research by professor Dan Gilbert; are we using someone else's mental map and cues to lead us to happiness! Spending time on Facebook has been shown to make many unhappy. We can't keep up with the surreal, best face forward Facebook postings. Everyone only puts his or her good stuff up, not the crap, boring real life events that actually fill our day. Everyone seems to be living amazing, happy lives. How can we compete and keep up with that? The quote by Theodore Roosevelt expresses what we have known about this happiness killer for a long time, "Comparison is the thief of joy".

As I learned from dogs, it's vital to understand that happiness is not derived from the outside; you don't get happiness, you generate it from within. And, because it can only be generated from within, happiness is a state of mind. It's all neuro chemistry! We can choose to be happy and then go about our day happily achieving. The best way I know to generate happiness within myself is by being grateful. By focusing on all the good things in my life, the people who I surround myself with, where I'm at in my current stage of life, who I've become as a person, the skills and knowledge I've learned and the few material things that make me happy. My bikes are wonderful at generating amazing experiences for me and I'm so appreciative of them for that. Dogs are following their heart, being true to themselves. They are as real and as authentic as it gets. Living for themselves not anyone else. At the end of their day they have a "good" tired from a day well spent. They seem to have a peace and a deep gratitude for their life. After all, as the saying goes, it's a dog's life!

Happiness can come down to contrast. If we keep comparing ourselves to those who have more, to the high standards that the media and Facebook portray, we will always feel like we aren't measuring up. Our car won't be fancy enough, our house won't be big enough, we won't be rich enough, our body won't be good enough and our life will seem too darn boring compared to Facebook. This will contribute to lower self-esteem, low mood and maybe even depression.

As you recognize, our modern society has really pushed for us to be and do better. We should be more successful, we should be striving to be happier, have better kids, better relationships, have six pack abs etc. Personal growth is a big business. But I want you to question this. As a thought maybe you should stop trying to be more successful. Maybe you should stop trying to be happy all the time. And maybe you should accept your kids and life as they currently are! Let all the guilt associated with holding on to this ideal world go as well.

Why would I say such a thing? It's all about contrast and the subconscious mind. What happens if you are constantly thinking that you should be happier, have more money etc. ? It starts to create self-doubt that you aren't happy now, that you don't have enough now and so on. It's sending a message to your subconscious that what you currently have isn't enough or good enough. I believe this constant striving for betterment can make us feel worse about ourselves. Do we need more guilt like this in our life?

The exciting thing about happiness is once it's born, you can nurture and grow it by discovering and adding on to it with other experiences that will bring you more joy, happiness and exhilaration. Go generate a new experience with your dog. Interact and work with them. Watch your dog run and play. Notice how they are focused in the present moment and how they have simplified the world. See how they are happily achieving as they go about their day. Think about how lucky you are to have them in your life. Surface those warm and fuzzy feeling of gratitude towards them and humans too!

So I will say it again, gratitude leads to happiness. I would suggest taking a good look around and start counting your blessings. Start seeing and finding the good. Start being appreciative of the things you already have, the people who are in your life, the wonderful place you live, the opportunities you have and the wonderful animals called dogs that you have in your life. That can make anyone happy.

Finding Meaning For Happiness

How much time a day do you focus on your happiness? Having spent so much time with dogs outside and in the woods I have observed that dogs are almost always happy when they are doing something. I think my dogs spent almost 100% of their time (other when they were sleeping) just being happy. Heck I think they're happy doing that as well. They enjoy playing because they weren't worrying about the future. They were simply enjoying the moment and the day. They are always full of curiosity and enthusiasm seeking out new and novel smells, new things to explore, new adventures, new places and things to discover and new dogs to play with.

As an observation, it seems dogs are happy just by themselves. They don't need other dogs to be happy; they can find happiness from within. However, they also take it to the next level of happiness and fulfillment when they are "working", when there is meaning to their play, when they are engaged with humans, i.e.: throwing the ball or stick, or herding, doing field trials or even obstacle courses. Working with their human, engaged in a job or activity seems to just take their happiness to the next level. It wasn't the job itself, rather, it seems it's the engagement and interaction with the human that gives them happiness. Having purpose and socializing at the same time seemed to be bliss for them. So what have I learned from this?

Circling back to the idea of happiness maps, maybe we may have been following an errant happiness map when it comes to our own happiness. I know I was. Why do I say this? According to the newest research in the field of positive psychology, happiness doesn't lead to meaning in your life. It's seems it may actually be the other way around. If we seek meaning then we find happiness. So for those who don't feel happy with their life currently, start looking for things that give you and your day more purpose and more meaning. As a side note, there is much data showing that it's not money that makes us happy at work. Rather it's if we feel appreciated and if we find our work meaningful.

What worked for me was asking myself over and over, what meaning and pleasure could I extract from what I'm doing today? What is the purpose of my daily tasks at my job? What results do they lead to? I question how my role fits into the bigger picture or scheme of things in my community and how the things I do impact others to help them in some bigger way.

What's important for me is I need to understand how my work impacts and serves others. How does it contribute to the betterment of the community? How does it impact my business and the world?

Again, it's this idea of shifting my thinking from, what can I get to what can I give and contribute that builds meaning in my day.

Let go of things that are not important to you. Slow down and simplify. Build your lifestyle around things that give you meaning, that you feel passionate about and this will lead to your greater happiness. Your dog will love going for a walk with you. Get more engaged with them. Work and stimulate their brain more with new learning experiences. Appreciate them more. It will be a win-win that will make both of you happier.

Keep Growing To Be Happy

I now believe we are stronger than what we think and that we are at our best when we are faced with and working on bigger challenges. They make us tap into our creative intelligence and internal resources. They stretch us and make us look deeper inside to find new insights about ourselves. They build new skills and let us tap into new resources to grow. We could look at them as a burden, something that holds us back or a gift, something that allows us to stretch, grow and build meaning into our life. How do you want these challenges to be for you? We can all chose!

Living in Ghetto Village I used to complain that I wanted life to be easier because it was hard for me. Now I would suggest that we don't wish that life were easier, wish that we were better! Then go about getting better and stronger. Develop more skills and more wisdom! Learn, grow, and develop yourself so you become bigger than your problems. We can become a bigger person so our problems seem smaller. And here is the amazing part, we can then go out and get some even bigger problems that will really help us stretch and grow. From the person living on the street to Warren Buffet they both have money problems, but the size of the problem is very different. Who's problem would you rather have? Thus it's not about getting rid of problems it's about getting new ones that make you grow in the ways you want.

We need the sense of progress leading towards some end goal thus, I believe in constant improvement in one's life. However, and this is the key, we should be striving for improvement out of curiosity and not out of societal pressure, family guilt or a sense of inadequacy or incompleteness in our life. I know I'm a bit weird this way, but I try and generate and develop an exciting and motivating curiosity for how I can grow in body, mind, and spirit. I wonder about how I can build deeper more fulfilling relationships. Can you envision a life like this for you? Again this helps build meaning in your life, which in turn leads to greater happiness. Moving towards a goal or end result that we find worthy is part of the human experience. It's part of what brings us true success and fulfillment.

True happiness comes from creating a whole life structure (lifestyle) that supports your true desires, deepest longings and overall health. It's the slow steady refinement of the people, the things, the circumstances and the environment that you choose to surround yourself with. It's not about who you are, rather it's about who do you want to be and then becoming that person. We are human becoming's.

Socialization is also vital for boosting happiness. In the chapter on socialization I built on the idea of how socialization, one of the key lessons I learned from dogs, is so important for our happiness and longevity. So call up some friends and go see them with your dog.

You Can Be Right Or Happy

Some people have this thing about being right. It's almost a "proving" thing as if they have to prove they're smarter or right. They might do this to build themselves up or to put others down. Or it could simply be a habit. Either way, it can drain joy and happiness from one's life. And it makes them a bummer to be around.

Going back to the key point, you can be right or you can be happy. I've found in life that you get what you focus on, and what you focus on expands! If you are always looking for fault, you will find it. And the more you look, the more you will find and it becomes a self-fulfilling circle. You will find what is wrong, incorrect, or inaccurate with things and people. It can become a "negative" non-supporting habit that can make you unhappy.

It would seem simple enough that to improve our relationships, to gain a greater sense of gratitude and fulfillment from life, to reduce our stress and to simply be happier we may need to relax a bit and not be so critical of others. To not always focus on finding the wrong details, rather look at the bigger picture of things and find the good.

It can be helpful to ask some empowering questions such as, what is good about what they are saying or doing? How can we use and benefit from this? I like to get curious and ask why they think that way or have that opinion. How can we learn, grow and utilize this to move ahead and not make same mistake again?

This comes down to controlling our mind and thoughts and choosing to find the good. To focus on the positive and what's right about situations, people and their actions. This sounds easy, but experience teaches that it's much harder to put into practice. Why?

Because we are animals of habit and old habits are hard to break. Combined with all the negative in the media, and many around us who are also negative, we are constantly reminded and bombarded with negative, fear mongering news. I understand this is a hard habit to break. But again, I turn to my dogs. They didn't do this; they seemed to just accept people and other dogs for who they actually were.

In the bestselling book entitled "The Power of Habit" by C. Duhigg he states that we can never break a habit. However, we can replace it with one that is more empowering and useful to us. But it takes acknowledgement of the non-supporting habit and then practice to implement and replace it with the new habit.

My experience has taught me that you can flip things around and make incredible dramatic changes very quickly by starting with three small, simple easy to do steps.

The first of which is choosing and deciding to find the good or the positive in others and yourself. This helps build and develop the skill of finding the good. Why do this in others first? Because, sometimes it's easier to find the good in others than it is in us. For everyone you meet always find one nice things about him or her and complement them on it. Soon, when you look in the mirror, you will start finding more good in yourself as well.

Shifting from being problem focused to solution based is another strategy. It is so easy to get caught up in finding fault and complaining. And as you know, like attracts like. Someone complains about the weather or traffic and shortly thereafter it's a pile on with horror stores of traffic hell. It's also easy to try and blame someone else for the situation or mess. It's easy to blame, complain or justify why something happened. Stop this. Instead step up and own it.

Take full responsibility for our life and shift our thinking to solutions. Don't let the things you can't do stop you from doing the things you can do. What can we do? What are some action steps we can take? Whose help can we get? What other information or resources do we need? Take action, make progress and move ahead.

Related to the point above, finding and thinking about negative outcomes is common, and it's a non-supporting habit that many develop. We will often make the statement "What if… fill in blank with negative". We can train our mind to shift this around to be more positive by converting this statement to. "What if… positive outcome inserted here".

To make this even better, follow it up with, "And what's the worst that could happen?" Usually this isn't too big of a deal. It also helps reduce any lingering fear or doubt. Ask others for their input and how they see the solution becoming a positive.

No one is perfect so why go there and try and find fault? What is it that we want to choose to do? Teaching and controlling our minds to find the good and expand on it takes time and practice until it becomes a habit. We can set ourselves up to win by surrounding ourselves with positive, like-minded people and look for the good! Start your day right with some positive, uplifting instructional material. I could suggest, taking your dog for a walk. See how happy they are. You are on your way to a happier more fulfilling life.

Dogs have this insatiable curiosity for life. They don't carry judgments and hurts and emotions from yesterday into today. They don't fret or worry about the past and they don't care about the future. They seem to know how to let it go. They live in the here and now. They are always present and focused right here, right now! They are living for this moment. And interesting enough, this seems to make them happy. Think about how much we can learn from them.

We can reflect and think about some things we should let go of, maybe we can forgive someone to allow us to move forward, we can look for ways to simplify our live so we are more focused and more grateful for what we have and who is in our life right now. We could start looking for the good in people and situations as we go about our day happily achieving. When we are socializing we could catch ourselves from drifting off and refocus ourselves to the other to be more mindful of the moment, to be present.

In how many positive ways would our life improve if we started reflecting on the meaning we find in our work and daily activities? How would finding more meaning in our daily activities make us happier? And what if we chilled out more and were a bit kinder to ourselves (and others) by giving ourselves more credit for what we do, how would that help shift the quality of our relationships and life?

And finally, what fun or new ways could we come up with to socialize more to further boost our happiness and fulfillment? What can we be thankful and grateful for today? When are you going for a walk with your dog so you can learn from the master of happiness? I'm sure it will lift your spirits. Don't you just love these animals!

LESSON 10
Love

When I had my first dogs Lady and Casy, my birthday was always a time for a special celebration. Lady was given to me on my twentieth birthday so it was a time to celebrate her coming into my life and all the positive changes that had come about because of this. In the summer of 1990 I was turning thirty; she had been with me ten years. And this year I had treated myself to something special on this birthday. I was giddy with excitement and awe. It was so very wonderful and special to me. Well built, all black with silver rings and it felt really good in my hands. It looked cool and I loved it. The potential it possessed was exhilarating to me. I was now going to be able to make and keep my memories of Lady and Casy. I got my very own SLR film camera. (Digital cameras weren't yet on the market.)

Now, my birthday is at the end of the August so as the fall rolled around on my walks in the woods I started taking pictures of the wonderful colours the maple trees turned. And it struck me one day, why didn't I ever notice the trees changing colours before? I'm sure it happens every year, but why didn't I notice it, why was this major environmental change not on my radar? How did I miss out on it for so long? I had just turned thirty and didn't have any real memories of the fall season and leaves changing colours! Where had I been?

One amazing thing this camera did was it taught me to see the beauty before me as well as to seek it out. There could be a whole forest in front of me of beautiful colours or if it was a bit later in the season, simply silhouettes of the trees, but if I zoomed in on just one part I could find some colours or patterns I found intriguing. In photography this is called optical isolation. This was a good lesson for me in finding the good. This is how I reflect upon and see love.

To me there is nothing else like love to take us to our highest elated highs or our lowest suffering lows. It can make life feel magical and seems to make it much more meaningful. It can surface a higher character and produce more empathy, compassion, kindness, and forgiveness in us. It takes us to a higher vibrational energy! We feel so connected and in turn, we resonate more of it back to the world.

The Abundance Of Love

My belief is that like Einstein's theory of relativity, that energy is neither created nor destroyed, and to that, love is not created or destroyed. We came into this world from love and thus I think love is always present, like a divine energy that flows freely through all of us. Yet for certain reasons we lose touch of it or cut it out of our lives. Or we just don't notice it and it fades out of our consciousness similar to the way we don't feel the watch on our wrist. It's still there in abundance but we just have to learn how to see and find it, and then let it into our lives.

All have been lifted to their greatest heights by love and all have been hurt by love. Some vow never again. Some want to hold onto the poison that love is bad or hurtful as they think this way of thinking helps. It doesn't. They just don't move on. They don't have the courage to open up to love again. It hardens their character. They close the door and build a wall around themselves to keep the hurt out.

Most people I have spoken to about this have shared a similar feeling. We have all felt we weren't cared for the way we might have liked; we didn't get the attention we so deeply craved. Others judged or rejected us and labeled us. (You know how kids can be with name calling!) And just think back to all of the stories, articles, TV shows and media blasting the message "protect your heart" that you have heard. What impact has that had on us? Over time we build up a wall to keep the hurt and pain out. There is a consequence to this though.

There is lots of love to go around for everyone but some have the idea that that love is limited and thus they think there is only so much to go around and so they're very cautious on how much they give out. And only doing so when they think it's safe. This generates the feelings of lack, contributes to hording and thus limits how much love they give to others. It decreases their desire to give love thinking they won't get any in return.

The sad tragedy is, this "conditioning" to protect our hearts starts when we are young, immature and confused about life. Building a wall to protect our heart also keeps out the thing we want the most, love. Regrets of the past, things we should have done, would have done, or could have done often are related back to love and our relationships.

I think we could all agree that more love in our life is a good thing. That it can make us more empathetic, connected, caring and emotionally fulfilled. Thus I have to wonder, is this why so many crave a dog in their life? They can let them in behind the wall and absorb all the unconditional love that dogs give without being vulnerable to the hurt others may impose upon them. Have we lost the courage to love openly again?

I had a personal experience with this. As you may know, your environment shapes you! It might be hard to understand, but mental illness can rip love out of a home. There wasn't much love in our house; on the contrary, there was a lot of anger, yelling and hate. As well, the lack of talking and communication contributes to a silence that can be deadly in destroying love in a family. I couldn't show signs of weakness or softness (emotions) living in the group home when I was a teen, or in the gangs I was in later on. I felt I was a hardened, troubled suburban trash street kid with a tough impenetrable shell to others feelings, and my own. I had zero empathy. I felt disconnected, ridiculed and rejected by life. Love was not to be found.

My time living in Ghetto Village in the early 80's further developed my negative mindset and contributed to a wall being built to keep more hurt and pain out. The lack of affection and caring from my parents and siblings, a broken heart from a first love gone, and the feelings of rejection from society developed this protection mindset of "don't get hurt again". My heart was torn out of my chest, I felt rejected and alone in a hostile and cold environment. I sure didn't think I was capable of being warm, kind, open and loving. I did what I thought was the right thing to do to protect myself; I built a wall to keep the hurt out. This mindset made me cold and slowly dimed my awareness of the love around me.

And just like you, I had lost love before and was hardened by heartache. Never again I thought. And like many, I believed I had to build a wall to prevent this from happening again. Your environment shapes you. It was just the way I was raised and the events that happened to me. It made me insensitive and cold to others and the world. My wall kept the hurt and love out. But there was some good news.

Having dogs in my life made me a more loving person and helped set the stage for a more loving life. How did dogs do this?

Similar to how the camera allowed me to "see" and find the beauty in my environment, having dogs allowed me to feel and then see the love that was actually present in my world. They initiated a desire for me to seek more love in my life. At this low point in my life, caring and compassion were the best ingredients for connecting with my dogs. It was a "safe" way to allow love into my life as well as express it. And this way of sharing emotions and love trickled over to my human relationships. Thank goodness for dogs!

Unconditional Love

Dogs are so wonderful in their ability to give unconditional love. Even though I was grumpy, yelled and scolded them, they must have saw something greater in me that I didn't see myself and they let all my poor behaviours and actions go. They were bringing something new out of me and I was helping them learn and grow. It was a win - win situation. We were giving each other the love we needed.

Their unconditional love and interest in me, their sunny spirits, insatiable curiosity and kindness quickly broke down my hardened shell. They somehow got under my skin and found a hidden passage to my heart that helped lift my spirits. Having them gave me a purpose and direction. My self-worth was so low I wouldn't do much of anything for myself to improve me, but I would do anything it seemed to help them develop and grow. And the more I did for them, the more our bond grew, and the greater my spirit was lifted. I became more compassionate, patient, forgiving, kind and grateful. I learned how to feel for them. I had empathy! This was something new for me. And, it was interesting to note how protective I became of them. I didn't want them to get hurt or injured. I was a good papa and protected them they best I could.

Having dogs made me response-able; they made me grow up. And in a unique way, they empowered me. As I put so much time into them I called them my "kids". And yes, I most definitely loved them. They gave me the love that I needed and in return I gave them a great life. I don't think I'm the only one who has had this experience. Most likely you have had these feeling and experiences as well. The modern world can be a cold place sometimes and dogs with their warm hearts, unconditional love and the ability to build deep social bonds with us seem to be doing their part to warm it up. Hurray for dogs!

Fur Babies

It was pretty obvious. I was seeing it all over social media and even on TV and in the gossip magazines so you know it's an "issue".

It struck me with intrigue and I had to ask the obvious question, why do all these young couples have dogs? Is there a gap in the flow of love from humans to humans thus many are feeling a lack of it? Are so many missing out on human love that dogs are now filling the gap? It seems to me that we are going to have a whole new generation of "Fur Babies"!

By the way, I'm not the only one who has called their dogs their kids. Maybe you've noticed this as well, but I have to ask the question based on my observations; have dogs replaced children in the modern family? As I've become older and approach sixty the trend is clear to me, dogs are replacing children in the up and coming twenty to thirty something's. Instead of having kids and their huge responsibility, many are starting "easy" with owning a dog and getting the unconditional love that we all want.

It seems the modern dog is fulfilling a different need than in past generations. In days past, having a dog was for protection, hunting, companionship or teaching the kids about the life cycle. Now they're surrogate babies! Are we lacking love that bad? And if so, is this a bad thing? I know having dogs at a critical time in my life sure changed my life. Have you noticed this trend as well?

At the dog park I've even heard people calling their dogs their "fur babies"? Further, just like what happened to me, these people are getting and building the skills and temperament for raising actual children in the future! I think they'll make great parents. Dogs are a great first step to parenthood. I just have to stop talking to our children in single one-word commands such as sit, stay, no…etc. Old habits die slowly! Similar to how some parents "spoil" their kids some are doing this with their dogs.

Some dogs are being treated better than humans! Some are taking this "dogs as kids" thing to new levels and spoiling them with multiple sleeping beds, toys galore and the outfits! Do you know what I'm talking about here? The crazy outfits that some buy or make to dress up their dogs? And the new style of dog shows aren't even for the best in breed anymore, no they're for wildest and craziest dressed up dogs. And some even take it to the next level and start their own YouTube Channel hoping to make their dogs the next "child superstar". This looks to be almost as intense as hockey parents wanting their kid to be the next Sidney Crosby! There's lots of pressure on those pups to perform! But I ask the question, is it only the younger crowd adopting dogs as their "kids"?

Since I'm nearing my sixth decade of life, many of our friends are becoming empty nesters as their kids take flight and leave the home.

They love the freedom, the quietness, and so much more for about two seconds. Then BOOM, they get a dog! Tell me, don't your friends or parents say these things? "The house is so big and quiet without them", "We were lonely without the kids", "I needed a reason to get outside and exercise more!" It just goes to show you the power of a warm heart, a fuzzy coat and big cute eyes! That loving and nurturing instinct keeps burning in us. And dogs do a great job of filling the gap. They just drink all the attention and love up. We have that need to nurture and give love and we need to feel love. Dogs are filling the empty nest when the kids leave home and continue to give us their unwavering love. What a great animal these dogs truly are. And so versatile, they fit in with all the crowds! Dogs are doing their part to break down the walls that can keep love out of our lives.

After our house fire in 1966 we moved to a small rental house close to the public school in Lindsay. My parents were away on vacation and trying to relax after our house had recently burnt down. Uncle Drew was there to look after us five kids. I was in the middle of the pack at five years old. Uncle Drew was just 18 and still a kid himself.

To stay out of trouble, we did what many little boys did; my older brother and I went fishing over at the tunnel. The tunnel was underneath a two-lane road about a fifteen minute walk away. It had cement pads on either side of the creek to help channel the water. These were great to set up our fishing gear on. We took our dog, Sidney, as company. She was a medium size dog with a slight build. Her fur was short and coarse. It was a light brown tan colour and she had white patches on her chest, paws and the tip of her tail. As little kids are, I became engulfed in worms, crayfish, hooks, running water and fishing. The rest of the world disappeared until the wail of a horn and skidding tires followed by a big thump and yelping. Sidney had been hit by a car! We rushed to her aid.

I ran as fast as my little legs would go to be with her. I wanted to help and comfort her but she was in pain. When I tried to help, she lashed out and bit me. This was the only way she knew how to express herself. As I discovered, this was an early lesson that also applied to people. I can't remember how but we got her home and to the vets. Thankfully Sidney wasn't severely hurt and allowed me to comfort her the next day. She forgot that she bit me, and I let the event go so I could move on. But it did mean a trip to the hospital for my bite wound.

I've observed this similar lashing out behaviour in humans. They get hurt by love, you try to help or comfort them, they don't let you in, and even lash out when we try to comfort them. For some reason they want to wallow or and stay stuck in past hurt from love. They've built a big wall around their heart. It's as if they don't want to heal or for some reason they find meaning or identify with the hurt. Dogs taught me to let stuff go and move on. They don't let past events keep love out. This doesn't mean we can't comfort and help them. It also doesn't mean we can't move on and open our hearts again to love. I just don't think we should let past hurts stop us from moving ahead in life. Some dogs are known as therapy dogs. Well, this could be a very useful form of therapy, healing the heart, don't you think?

Tough Love

Ah, tough love; the discipline to say no when you really want to say yes to something is a skill we all seem to have problems with. What seems to be so simple, yet is so hard to apply, is that of tough love. Thankfully, dogs taught me much about this lesson and helped to build up my "tough love muscle" that I have applied many times and have shared with our children. I wish I had learned this lesson when I was younger.

There were almost no rules in our home when I was growing up in the 60's and 70's. My parents were very liberal post 60's hippies and freedom was king. I did what I wanted when I wanted for almost my whole life up to this point. Some might use the word wild to describe me. At age 12 if I wanted to stay out all night I just did. If I wanted to eat junk food I did. If we wanted to drink, we stole the booze from someone's parents and just did. I didn't like school so I didn't go much. There were almost no repercussions. And the few rules that were enforced were lame, non-instructional and did nothing to alter my behaviour. As you can imagine, this lead to worsening escapades in my behaviour and many-many trips to the police station and juvenile court.

The juvenile judge now recognized me by sight. At this "meeting" he vigorously announced from behind his big desk, "Mr. Ridpath, you are on a bad path and we have to put a stop to it. Your behaviour needs to be reeled in. We have to apply some tough love". This was my "ticket" to being removed from our family home and entrance to living in a boy's group home. I guess the judge was giving me some tough love to help straighten me out. I think he was right in his actions.

Lady and Casy were my first dogs in my early twenties. Having them taught me much about this tough love thing. We lived near a very busy intersection in the Toronto suburbs. Both dogs would always heal closely beside me when I walked even without a leash attached. However, I now deeply cared about these animals and I didn't want them to get hit by a car so I always kept them on a tight leash near the roads or sidewalks. I know this saved their lives many times. Animals can be unpredictable and get distracted by things like squirrels, thus lurching away faster than you could ever respond so you have to be ready for these situations. I had to apply tough love to keep them safe. They had to stay on the leads.

If you have owned dogs you know this scenario. Sometimes the dogs would come across a dead animal or even garbage and start to eat part of it. This would inevitably cause them to get the "poops", aka diarrhea! Yuck! To help them get over this I would hold off feeding them and fast them for a day. This sounds easy yet the whining and begging, which was pretty incredible some days, was hard to overcome and could easily break you down ultimately pulling you away from the end goal at hand. I had to be strong and stay firm to my commitment of not feeding them for the day. This was the best thing for them even though they didn't understand or appreciate it. They most likely thought I was some mean owner! Tough love was applied.

Dogs don't buffer their emotions the way humans do. When a female dog comes into heat her hormones take over, reason goes out the window, a deep drive to reproduce follows and trouble, aka puppies, can ensue. Any rational thoughts the dog may have had vanish! For this short period of time it's important to keep them separated from the males. My experience taught me that they could get very creative and become incredible escape artists.

Lady had the surgery first at about six months of age, but due to money issues Casy didn't get spayed (fixed) until she was about 2 years old so there were a few times when she was receptive. When she went into heat I had to keep her on a leash, inside the house or in the very small fenced back yard where I thought she would be "safe". It was a relatively tall fence at about four feet tall but this was nothing for a tall frisky athletic dog with one thing on her mind! It was difficult being the stern, fun busting, authoritative "dad" but it had to be done. I often felt guilty keeping her in yet I knew it was the right thing to do. Keeping her apart from the male dogs was tough love.

When it came to putting Max down the same tough love was applied. I wanted to keep him around for us, and the love he gave us, but I also knew he was suffering. The vomiting, diarrhea, kidney failure, toxemia, and the pain had reduced the quality of his life to rock bottom. His vitality was gone. It was his time to go but I felt it wasn't my time to let him go. I wasn't ready to say good-bye, but it had to be none. We applied some tough love and did what was best for him. Applying tough love was… tough! But the lesson it taught me serves me well to this day.

Desirable Difficulties

I first heard of the concept of desirable difficulties in Malcolm Gladwell's book entitled David and Goliath: Underdogs, Misfits and the Art of Battling Giants. This is a concept in learning put forth back in 1994 by Robert Bjork. The concept might sound counter intuitive at first glance but it works. He suggested that making learning tasks easy doesn't necessary lead to better learning. Making things hard on yourself, but in good way, creates desirable difficulties to enhance learning. Our brains tap into our creative intelligence and deeper resources to find solutions.

One example is that of dyslexia. There is a group of entrepreneurs with dyslexia who have been enormously successful. From the outside, many would think having such a challenge would limit their potential for success, however these people often state that they are successful not in spite of their disability, but because of it. For these people, they view their disability as desirable. It made them tap into their creative intelligence, helped build new and novel skills and accelerated their adaptions to their environment.

If we make learning too easy, people may not tap into their true creative resources or live up to their full potential. We may simply coast along and not tap into our deep innate resources. Having challenges makes us grow and develop more of our skills. There seems to be a limit though. If the difficulties are too extreme and difficult or if we have too many difficulties then it can impede learning. Each of us will have our own sweet spot for optimizing our growth.

Doing things that are demanding, things that take some deeper creative thought and skill, the things that are "tough" to do, build character and grit as well as develop the all-important creative intelligence. It helped me mature and taught me how to "walk on my own two feet". Do you want your kids to have it better than what you did growing up? I do. I don't want them to have the struggles and challenges that I went through but at the same time, I know how important it is to have challenges, setbacks, failures, the all-important "learning experiences" etc. as this is the foundation for building our internal resistance. It also helps build our life and coping skills. It helps us tap into and build our creative intelligence for problem solving. It builds resilience and grit. But, where is this balance found? I often struggle with this issue with our children. I want to help them out but I don't want to make it too easy for them. I don't want to be the mean old dad from hell but I do want them to build their skills and coping resources. Am I being too easy on my kids? Am I not applying enough tough love? This is a constant struggle for me to find the right balance of tough love.

Work It Out - Or A Time Out?

I've noticed a social shift in the current parenting style that makes me feel uneasy. To me, I'm not sure of this modern parenting style of coddling kids and protecting them from every possible bump or bruise, be it physical or emotional. It doesn't seem to be a good idea to me. I wonder if we are over parenting. Are we being too involved and "helicoptering" around too much and not allowing the kids to struggle and dig a little deeper into their own internal resources to solve problems? Are we giving them too much handholding? Are we turning them into marshmallows? I have even heard this new generation being called "snowflakes" as they don't have the internal resistance, creative intelligence, fortitude or grit to carry on when faced with the typical life problems. Yikes, that is really scary for them!

Because of this over parenting are they missing out on developing some of the key life skills needed to get by and thrive? Have we taken away too much of the "desirable difficulty"? And lastly, I wonder why are we afraid to let the kids grow and develop? We seem to be ok with letting dogs play and horse around and work it out with the other dogs but not so with our kids. It almost seems that there is a fear of letting the kids do it themselves in case they… fail! Oh my gosh, what would happen to their poor little egos? How could they survive such a blow?

If they aren't learning these lessons when they're young when the consequences are small, when are they learning them and will the consequences be more severe and impactful at a later stage in life? Coming back to the idea of love, are we developing a generation of kids who are overly dependent on us, their parents? Are we doing this for their sake or our sake, to satisfy our desire to be needed, wanted, useful and loved? I have to ask, do we want these kids to be more dependent on us for our own personal reward? Or is it a different reason?

We all seem to be caught up in our own online world that we don't communicate and connect with real live people the way we used to. The way we most likely need to base on our biology, social needs and heritage. Are we all so alone and lacking love that dogs with their unlimited supply of unconditional love and dependency on us are now filling the gap? Are they our new "fur babies"?

We let our dogs work it out so why don't we let the kids work it out? I've noticed kids can't just go and make up games in the park anymore. They can't simply use a tree and a coat for the goal posts. They need all kinds of fancy hi-tech gear. We used to make up the teams, the rules and we got along. We played and had fun. Were there problems and even fights? Absolutely, but we worked it out and got on with it. We didn't need therapy just because we didn't get picked for the good team! Some were better than others and not everyone won! If you weren't that good, to get better you looked up to the better kids and tried to emulate and learn from them. You practiced the skill necessary for growth and improvement. That was life in the playground. Our parents weren't there trying to make sure things were fair and everyone got along!

Yet now, everything has to be structured and supervised by parents. When playing games we used to work it out, now with all the structured play the kids just get a time out! Why are there no losers, only winners? Why do we praise them when we don't really mean it? Or why do we give them credit for having inherent ability? Isn't that setting them up to fail later in life? Are we being too nice? Are we afraid to hurt their sensitive little feelings in fear of "scarring" them for life? Are we not applying enough tough love?

Similar events unfold in the dog parks. You've seen this before. Maybe the bigger dogs are stronger, but the smaller dogs learn different strategies that optimize their size to keep away from them when they play. The larger taller dogs play bite on top of the neck, the smaller dogs go for the front legs, the belly or maybe even the tail! Some are faster; some are more agile, yet each learns to play to their strengths and advantages as they build their skills. Sometimes they bite too hard and the other yelps and bites them back even harder to send the message, "Hey that hurt and this is what it feels like. Don't do that again!" They most often just work it out and a natural hierarchy develops. But common sense isn't always common practice in us humans.

Why is it that we need to be told not to let our ten-year-old children take their phones to bed? Was I over reacting when I got mad (blew a gasket) when my daughter told me she didn't sleep well because her friend was texting her at 3am! Honey, why are you taking your phone to bed and why are you answering a text at 3am? I had to apply some tough love (common sense!) and not allow her to do this anymore! We took the phone away at night. The lesson of tough love was an important lesson for me to learn and I use it all the time with my children!

We had only had Max for four or five months. The sun felt warm on our faces. It was a bright sunny spring day. The grey and gloomy clouds of the winter had finally blown away; the birds were back and singing wildly. It was the spring of 2011. The snow had finally melted and the ground was waking up. The trails were mostly dry. We could hear the grit of the sand below our shoes as we walked along the sidewalk near the road. Max was pulling hard at the leash, and he wanted to run. Jody was still young, about ten years old, and was having a difficult time keeping him under control. With the cuteness and innocence only children have she asked me in an excited but soft gentle voice "Max really wants to run dad. Can I let him off the leash now?" I answered her with a question and applied some tough love.

Do you love Max and do you want to keep him safe? I asked. She gave me a spirited Yes! I enquired again; more than anything you know he wants to be let off the leash to just run, chase squirrels and be free now, right? Again she said yes. What would happen if there was a squirrel on the other side of the road and he ran after it, he may get hit by a car on the road and get killed right? I dug deeper into her reasoning; So, what should we do? Should we let him off or keep him on the leash? Keep him on she timidly stated. I dug just a bit deeper to confirm her answer. Even though he really, really wants to run and chase the squirrels more than anything do you think we should keep him on the leash? Her response was immediate. She knew what had to be done. She applied some tough love. Yes. Lets keep him safe until we get to the park.

Somehow these animals get under your skin and deep into your heart. Their forgiving nature, unconditional love, deep devoted loyalty, funny little antics and quirkily little mannerisms that make us uncontrollably laugh and cry all contribute to the deep bond of love we form with them.

When I was twenty, in my lowest low, they somehow broke down the wall I had build up around my heart to keep hurt out. They allowed me to realize that there is an unlimited supply of love in the world but we just have to become aware of it and let it flow into and from us. They also taught me the importance of tough love which has served me so often. These lessons have been so vital in my personal growth. I feel fortunate and grateful that I learned them. How lucky am I? How lucky are you to have these wonderful animals in our life.

Through the ups and downs of my life I've often had to ponder many times about my limiting beliefs. I think to myself, is there anything in my life that I'm holding on to that's preventing love from coming into my life? Is now the time to let go of it and move on and make room for the future? Is now the time to chip away at the wall or barrier that's keeping love out of my life?

What did I find that works for me? Go pat a dog, spend time with them seeing how they interact with the world. Just being around them and seeing how they give unconditionally of love will lift our spirits. Better yet, get a dog to help breakdown the wall and let the love shine in again. And don't be afraid to let love flow forth from you, there is lots to go around. You and I deserve and are worthy of love. We all are. Dogs are a great example of this, lets learn from them.

When they come into our lives they steal our hearts. When they leave, they tear it out. Love is an important ingredient in the life cycle of dogs.

LESSON 11
The Life Cycle

When they come into your life they steal your heart... When they go, they tear it out. Ah, there is that line again. If you've owned a dog, you know how true this is and its true impact is clearly felt when we say good-bye to our furry animal friends.

The little black lab puppy named Lady came into my life on my twentieth birthday. Her coat had an incredible shine to it. Her ears were so very soft, like velvet and they flopped over her ears at rest and perked up when she was intrigued. Her eyes were big, brown and looked deep into my soul. She was a playful dog; a bit shy, really athletic and extremely smart. She loved being in the woods nose to the ground or in the park doing and learning new tricks or chasing squirrels. She was a loving, faithful dog very devoted to us. Her kindness and love helped take me on a new path in life. A path I would never have dreamed possible for me.

With her "sister" Casy, we had so many wonderful memories together. Taking the ferries and going to Toronto island, camping, travelling through Toronto on the buses, streetcars and subways, all the fun trips to High Park, tobboganing in the winters, I threw sticks and balls so many times I could have made it as an outfielder for the Jays and of course all the time we spent in the woods and ravines playing by the rivers, chasing squirrels, or groundhogs. Fifteen years is a long time for a dog.

Saying Goodbye

I blinked. Where had all the time gone? It was 1995 I was now almost thirty-five and I was going to be getting married soon. My wife to be, Heather, and I would be going away on a honeymoon for a few months to South America. Lady needed extra attention, more patience, special food and the arthritis had made her sore and weak. She was 15 years old. I felt that her time was up. She was my first "child", given to me on my twentieth birthday by a good friend. This dog was incredibly special to me. Her presence in my life changed everything for me. We went through so much together, the years of struggles and hard times and now the good times. She was always there by my side. My running partner, faithful loyal companion and best friend to Casey. Saying good-bye and death is an inevitable consequence of having a dog unless they outlive you. I have wondered if they would miss me the same way I miss them.

 I was looking for a sign so I had an excuse not to play GOD. In reality, it was a justification to ease my guilt of putting her down. I knew I was going to have to say goodbye and put her down before the wedding. But I just couldn't think about it. There was no way I would have the emotional strength to do it. This was my "kid". This dog had changed my life and given me so much. I was so in debt to her. Then it came, deep red blood in her urine. Her kidneys were failing. It was time.

 I made the appointment at the vet, prepaid the bill and went home. I was going to be an emotional mess and wanted to take care of the paperwork beforehand. Two more days with her, how do you prepare for this? They don't know what's going to happen. You can't tell them and prepare them. In reflection, I don't think they need it the way we humans do. I gave her some extra treats, we had a few longer walks and I was as kind and gentle with her as I knew how to be. I kept her by my side for two days always patting her and telling her what a good dog she was. I was preparing myself the best way I could to say goodbye.

 Over the almost six years I worked at the animal hospital I had to help put many animals down for various reason. I had seen many die of injuries and natural causes. I thought I was cool with the death and dying thing and could handle it. Not so. I had no idea how this was going to tear my heart out. If you have ever had to say goodbye to a dog or pet you know what I'm talking about. The joy, affection and love that these animals give us pales to what we do for them. Time goes by so fast and we don't even know it. Sneaky.

 The day came. I took her to the clinic and they put us in a quiet room. The vet came in as prearranged and administered the medication as I held her. I was shaking like a leaf. It was done. Saying goodbye was mentally retching. I was so stirred. What had I done! It tore my heart out. I cried for her passing and my sadness and loss. This was my second exposure to this life lesson and truly solidified my understanding of the life cycle.

My other dog, Casey had to be put down just a few months earlier in an emergency situation due to a gastric torsion in her stomach. She too was close to 15. That was a quick emergency situation with two options; emergency surgery that may or may not save her life or put her out of pain and misery with euthanasia. I didn't have time to stew on it. I just did the right thing for her. It wasn't really a choice. I used tough love and did the right thing. I came home and cried. Lady kept barking as if to say "Where are you? Come on out and play." The house was almost empty without her. We missed her presence so much. Her size and spirit had filled the void so well.

Over the following months and years I have reflected often on the lessons of the life cycle. I've lost dogs that were very close and dear to my heart. I've also lost family members. My youngest brother had died nine years earlier as had my brother-in-law and grandparents. So I get it, I've felt the loss and pain of both. I can't find the exact words to fully describe the difference between how I've felt when my dogs have passed vs. when humans close to me have passed. I'm afraid to share that as some may judge me the wrong way. Time goes by so fast and we don't even seem to be aware of it. Sneaky.

The shorter life span of dogs allows us to get the full picture of the life cycle, birth to death with all the ups and downs in between. They bring joy and elation when they come into your life and sadness and heartache when they leave. We cry and languish with their loss but for most their spirit continues to live on in our hearts and the pictures we keep of them. There are so many lessons to be learned from the amazing experiences of owning a dog.

Having dogs has taught me that yes indeed life is short and it goes by quick. I also now more fully appreciate when people state how fragile life and the human body is. But the biggest lesson and "aha moment" that dogs taught me is that of being present to the here and now, the lesson of being present in the moment. I wonder if they know that life is short and time is precious thus they don't worry about yesterday or fret about tomorrow and thus truly live in the day, in the moment.

Early in my life I was so hard and mean to myself. I believe that all of us can be hard on ourselves and often we judge ourselves too harshly with very little forgiveness or without the chance of a second look. Good news though, we have choices!

With deeper reflections on my life and the events that happened to me I realize now that many of the happenings were not always the way I thought they were. You see, our interpretations of the events that happen to us are surrounded by emotions that also cloud the meaning we read into events. Often when we are young we interpret the events through our underdeveloped mind and underdeveloped emotions. These meanings or interpretations stick with us, unchallenged in most cases through our life, and can be non-supporting as well as disempowering.

The early part of my life was highly emotionally charged in a negative way and thus I was interpreting the events through the lens of these negative emotions. And the kicker that was messing me up, I didn't realize or understand the "true" meaning of an event at that current moment in time. However, you and I can go back and re-evaluate and add or change the meaning we gave to this event by looking at it through the lens of more supporting emotions of a more mature person.

We can choose to apply any meaning we want to the event so it empowers and supports us. That is the power of the human mind. We can break the chains that hold us back and move freely into a more supporting and positive future. We can close this chapter of our life and with a clean slate, write the next chapter of life and live into the story we want to live… if we choose to.

Stay Young At Heart

Most of us were in our mid-fifties at this particular summer gathering. There was lots of laughter and hoots of glee as we were sharing stories about our aches and pains. The joys of getting older! One well put together women stated she walked by a door and wondered who the old lady was starting at her from the other room? It was a mirror and it was her reflection starting back at her! What a shock. She couldn't believe it. I still feel like I'm in my twenties she lamented. I can't see myself being this old! She closed that conversation by stating, "I might be getting old but I want to stay young at heart". This is what I've observed in dogs, they stay young at heart. Time goes by so fast and we don't even seem to be aware of it. Sneaky!

There is on old saying and assumption about getting older. It's a belief from days gone past that still permeates our culture, and it could be one of those limiting beliefs that is holding us back as we age. You've heard it many, many times before; "You can't teach an old dog new tricks!" Really? Where did this saying come from? I have a question for you, are you open to learning and growing? Can you still learn new things? If so, read on, you might not be over the hill yet!

First of all, are you an old dog? What is "old" anyway? If you are a teenager, anyone over 25 is over the hill. If you're 75 years old, 95 is "old" in relation to you. And what are the "tricks" you are suppose to be learning anyway? How about bounce around in circles on your legs and bark as someone holds a cupcake over you? Jump Robbie!

There may be physical limitations to what we can do however we can still work our mind. We can keep learning and growing, developing our perspective and understanding as well as building our all-important wisdom. At the know it all age of twenty, my mom once said to me; "I should be learning something new every day until the day I die. And on that day, I would learn about the life cycle and dying." I reminded her of this the last time I saw her before she passed. We can keep learning and growing until our last days.

When we got our first dog Max for our own children I wanted to shift the responsibility of taking care of him over to them as quickly as possible. We would often watch dog training shows on TV, talk about the "lessons" that the trainer would have to teach the owners to get their "bad" dog under control. We then shared how we all should apply the lesson to "their" dog Max.

An interesting pattern emerged. It seemed that many of these "troubled" dogs who were not stimulated or socialized during the day were the ones that were labeled the "bad" dogs. Often, they were left alone most of the day, not stimulated with not much else to do but chew on themselves or the furniture!

It was always great to see how these dogs turned around and became very different animals with greatly improved behaviour. What magic did the trainers apply? Lots of walks, interactions with other dogs (socializing) and mental stimulation were the primary ingredients to turn them around. The trainers often called "working" the dog a key transformation exercise. It's not physical work they were referring to, rather it was mental stimulation of their brains. They were working their brains, getting them engaged in life and their surroundings. Dogs love and need to learn, and I believe, so do humans or we go squirrely.

We all know the importance of exercise for healthy aging, but do we all get the importance of keeping our minds active for healthy aging? With dogs having a shorter and accelerated life, we can see this unfold within our own lives often over just one decade. With all my dogs I've kept them active and mentally stimulated. Yes there came a point where they couldn't run as fast or as far, but I still worked them (stimulated their brains) on the playgrounds and other obstacles. I hid balls, sticks or treats for them to find. I had them do the different obstacles in new patterns or backwards to help teach them new "tricks". I would hide and have them smell me out. I kept taking them to new and novel areas for their walks so they would have access to new experiences. My goal was to keep their life interesting and keep them engaged in living. I didn't want them to develop doggie brain mush! In humans we know this as dementia and cognitive decline.

Living and working with dogs has taught me to live more in the now, to be more present and to appreciate the now. I think we have to take advantage of our time here together. Be present for each other. Be here, in the now! Stay young at heart and don't grow up too fast. And lets not make our kids do this either. We may have blown it for us, so lets teach them some new more supporting ways of being.

My time with dogs tells me that they too must feel this way. Their bodies age and wear out but their spirits and enthusiasm for the day combined with the insatiable curiosity for each day keeps them young at heart. Even in Max's last few moments as we surrounded him to say goodbye, his tail kept waging as we softly whispered his name, "Hey Max, good dog. Good boy". If I had asked if he wanted to go for a walk, he would have dragged himself off that matt and headed for the door, turned and looked at me and given me the look of "Lets go!"

Another big lesson for me has been to make the best of each day. Make each day special. Don't just make it through the day; take from the day as much as you can. Squeeze it for all its juice. Make the memories. Build a rich library of experiences and "moments" that will fill your mind and heart for the rest of your time. I find this one hard to consistently apply. With life seemingly so busy it sometimes gets lost and put on the back burner.

Goodbye Max

I blinked again. Twenty more years have gone by, I'm now fifty-five as the mirror reminds me. It was early spring and a Sunday night - late. Things had really deteriorated over the last two weeks. He was splat out on the floor unable to muster the energy to get up or move. And, there was more diarrhea with gut retching vomiting. The smell was terrible but it didn't bother me. Listening to his moaning and gasping I knew. It was now so very clear in my mind. All of our good times were coming to an end. The walks, skiing in the woods, throwing the stick, chasing rabbits and squirrels, drying his feet after each walk, him doing tricks for treats, the comfort and companionship as he put his head on my feet watching TV, his begging and whining hoping for a bite as we carved the turkey, his rambunctious antics and games with our kids. It was ending. Max was dying.

I had to do one of the toughest things I've ever done in my life. I had to make the call, for him, for his sake. This wasn't right to see him suffer through this anymore. It was time to say goodbye to my dear friend, my shadow and my little buddy. I've even proclaimed "Max was the son I never had!" My heart was being torn out. I knew for a while this point would come but I wasn't ready to say goodbye and probably never would be. I don't think any amount of preparation really prepares you for these things. Time goes by so fast and we don't even seem to be aware of it. Sneaky!

Dr. Barb was right in her prediction of how this was going to unfold. His kidneys were now almost completely shut down. His blood was becoming a toxic cesspool that was altering how his brain was working. His blood cells couldn't transport oxygen very well so he had incredible fatigue. He lost this appetite and these toxins were making him highly nauseous and smelly. The quality of his life was deteriorating so very fast. He would have moments when I would think, "Oh, he's going to pull though". It wasn't to be. This genetic kidney defect (kidney disease) was running its course. The average life span of dogs with this condition is about 3 years. This would hold true for Max. He was to live for just over 3 years.

Telling the kids the next morning created another sea of tears. Max was their dog. They worked and persuaded Heather and I for at least a year to get one. They offered to pay for him. They picked him out of eleven or so other puppies. They named him; they walked, fed and cleaned him. He slept on their backs or in their laps or on their feet when he was young. They were all growing up together, learning the lessons of life together. Best friends and buddies. We all wanted to keep him around for our own selfish reason; companionship, unconditional love, cheap source of laughter and fun, and company when others were not around. But this was not about us. This was about him and how he was now suffering. The time had come so quick! Max had completed his lifecycle. He was dying. And now, we had to say goodbye!

They didn't have rooms like this at the clinics I had worked at. This was really nice. Not quite a hotel room, but a nice room, with a nice thick carpet, pictures of dogs and cats on the walls, some nice wood trim. It had a calm warm vibe. This was a nice comfortable place to say goodbye to a dear friend. Max was on the carpet as Dr. Barb put an IV catheter into his front leg. This would make it easier to inject the drug that stopped his heart. Heather, Jenna, Jody and I gathered around speaking in soft, quiet reassuring voices to him. We stroked his wonderful golden fur coat, pulling at some of his curls. Dr. Barb asked if we were ready to say goodbye. We all nodded. I looked deeply into his big brown eyes and said his name over and over. Max, Max, Max. He went limp and folded into our arms. Casanova was gone.

The next thirty minutes or so were very important in my life with Max. We cried for our loss of a wonderful animal. And then we smiled as we started remembering all the good times and the ways he brought joy into our life. The day we picked him up and how he threw up in the van on the way home. How he would climb into the laundry basket full of warm clothes fresh out of the dryer. How he made the residents at the seniors home light up as they patted him and remembered dogs from their past. The walks, skiing, runs, stick-throwing sessions and yes, even the times he was sick. Cleaning his always-dirty ears. Spraying him down sometimes several times a day in the spring when the ground was warming up and still very muddy. These stories made me realize how valuable dogs are in the modern human family life. The life lessons they can teach us, the skills we develop as we look after them, the emotions they develop in us are so valuable to all family members. They make us be better social pack animals! Max was a wonderful dog and so important in our lives. We miss him dearly.

Having dogs in my life has taught me so much about the life and death cycle. It's made me be more cognizant and realistic about my time here. It's taught me to value each day as a gift and that it's important to be present, to be in the now, not worrying about the past or fretting over the future, and how this being present can make you feel alive. They taught me the lessons of letting it go and not holding grudges or being bitter. This skill can lead to much greater joy and happiness in one's life. They broke down the wall I had built around my heart so I could let their love and other's love in and let the love in me flow out. Dogs are amazing and our time with them goes by fast. Time goes by so fast and we don't even seem to be aware of it. Sneaky!

In case you haven't noticed, time flies by! If there's something you want to do, I would suggest you do it now. If you feel there's someone inside whom you want to be, I would suggest you work towards being that person now. If there is something really special that you want, I would suggest going for it now. An important lesson that I've learned is, when it comes to the really important things in your life don't wait until tomorrow or put it off, because tomorrow may not show up. If you want inner peace, more loving relationships, happiness or whatever else, I would suggest that you start being happy now by practicing being what you want.

As I shared with you in the early chapters about my life, my teen years and yearly twenties were full of many upheavals. A few times in my life I have ended up in deep rut and came close to the edge. I didn't know how to get out of it and felt there was no help or hope. The burden was too great for me and my internal reserve was empty. I wanted to simply let go. Each time I was deeply troubled about not having lived fully, and not having lived up to my potential. This stirred me in profound ways as I knew I hadn't given enough attention to the true priorities in my life, my family, my health, my inner spirit, and I hadn't really taken enough time to play and have fun. I had let too many of my good friendships fade away.

I felt like there was still so much inside of me that I just wanted to bring out, nurture and share with the world. I felt incomplete having not fulfilled this desire. There was still so much I wanted to see and do! I vowed that if I ever got back on my feet and out of this mess, I would make changes for the better; I vowed that from here on, I would lighten up and enjoy the good simple things that abound me. I'd go after my true goals, enjoy the journey and live with peace and joy instead of stress and struggle. I'd never waste another day or take it for granted. I would view each day as a gift. I would take as much as I can from the day instead of just wasting time getting through it. I'm trying to apply all the wonderful lessons my dogs taught me each day. This has become my inner compass. What's guides you?

Having dogs has taught me two related lessons that have served to help me cleanse my soul and lift my spirit. Learning how to let things go so I can move on with my life and how to be more appreciative and grateful for all the wonderful things and people that are in my life right now. These are wonderful lessons that help to enrich my life.

LESSON 12
Gratitude and Letting It Go

The spring was finally here and the days were becoming warmer and most importantly for me, sunnier. I needed the sun to lift my spirits. The spring of 1981 was here which meant more time cleaning the dogs after our walks and it seemed we were always wiping off their feet. But I made it. The last eight months of living in Ghetto Village were brutal. So much had happened. I'm not sure how I made it through these last months with so much upheaval going go in my life, it felt like I had lived an emotional roller coaster from hell, but I made it. I gave credit to Lady and Casy for keeping me above ground. Being around them and working with them was really helping we navigate through these unsettled times. I was now getting a bit more understanding about the ideas of gratitude and why it was so vital to let some stuff go.

The dogs always grew thick winter coats to keep them warm in the winter but it got hot for them in the house. Casey liked to flop out near the front door to catch some of the draught that came in under the old tattered door to help cool her. It was close to 2 am. I was coming home after a long night of delivering Chinese food. I was tired and groggy. With no real thoughts in my head I just pushed open the door not thinking about who was going to be on the floor on the other side.

Her high pitch yelp startled the tiredness out of me. The door had pinched her foot as I swung it open. She was shaken and hurt. I got down to her level and comforted her, rubbing her foot and speaking kindly telling her that I was sorry and things would be ok. I took her out for a short walk. She forgave me and let this go. She didn't hold a grudge against me, she didn't try to get back at me, she simply let it go. That was the end of the story. She moved on.

This wasn't the only time things like this happened to the dogs. Others or I had stepped on their paws by accident, I had fallen back on them squishing them, I had stopped quickly in the car and they went flying forward (where are the doggy seatbelts?) and there were the many times I yelled at and scolded them. I was angry and maybe even mean and I took some of this out on them, which wasn't fair, but it was my only way of dealing with situations at this time. In all of these different circumstances they let things go and moved on. No grudges, no resentment, no judgment, and no bitterness, they just moved on. The contrast between how they forgave me and my lack of empathy and gratitude made me step up to their level and raised my appreciation of the importance of forgiveness. Thank goodness for dogs.

As I have observed, dogs don't judge us on our size, colour, or shape, just our actions and behaviour's, and sometimes our smell. They see our real character through our faults and accept us for who we are at our core. They see through our "human image", the one we try to impress other humans with. Our real character is revealed to them by our actions and behaviour not by superficial traits. They don't care about our designer clothes or fancy cars. This is part of the unconditional love and deep loyalty they have to us, their owners and caregivers.

Another wonderful thing about dogs is they don't hold grudges. They are able to let yesterday go. They forgive and forget and simply move on to now, the present, the here and now. They don't hold a grudge and hate you if you opened the door and banged them by accident or stepped on their foot as you get up from the dinner table. And, they don't hold it against you if you yelled at them yesterday. They don't care if you were in a poor mood yesterday, or whatever else, they just focus on the new day and the present moment. They let that other stuff go. There is so much I learned from them on gratitude, forgiveness and letting go. I couldn't really see the difference in myself at this point and thus I couldn't fully appreciate the true value of these lessons until a bit later in my life. These lessons I learned from my dogs I would say were transformational for me in my later years.

Working with my own dogs and the animals in the animal hospital I was learning so much about these fundamental lessons of life; letting it go and forgiveness. I was beginning to understand how they could reduce much anger, frustration, bitterness and remorse in us. Having the dogs around made me so much more appreciative of their special traits, company and insights. I was feeling very indebted and grateful to them for being in my life and helping me get by.

Interesting enough though, I've observed that some humans aren't always so forgiving. They seem to carry this baggage of grudges and resentment through their lives. They must have incredible strength to carry the weight of this burden. I must ask a simple question though, why would you want to? Why not let it go and offer forgiveness and reduce the load and stress in your life? Why not heal the past and move forward with a clean slate in your life? Why are they keeping score? I don't get it.

When my emotions are high or when I'm in a state of upheaval, letting go is such an important lesson to know and has served me well many times in my life including when we had to say goodbye to our dogs and when my mother and father were dying.

Let It Go

Her birthday was November 4 and in 1998 she was turning 65. Mom was now going to be retired and she was going to be moving into a condo building where my older brother and sister were living. Here, she would have more support from all of us and we thought, be much happier. The last few decades had been tough on her with my dad losing it and the family breaking up. Finally things were picking up and nicely coming together for her until today.

On the day of her sixty-fifth birthday almost like a bad joke, my mother was diagnosed with terminal bone cancer. It would take her quickly. Two months later in January 1999, near the end of her battle she was hospitalized as the cancer had spread through her body. Now she only had a few days to live. Yet for some reason the doctors decided to put her through a surgery that would put a metal rod down the hollow part of her leg bone, to stabilize it.

After the surgery, when I came to see her, she was drugged up and sleeping. Since I had nothing to do I read her chart. I noticed they hadn't fed her for almost four days before the surgery. When the surgeon came in I asked why they didn't feed her for so long? He told me I shouldn't read her chart and put me off. I then asked why she had the bone surgery. He replied, "To help stabilize her leg for when she gets back up walking". My response was heated, as I knew she only had a few days left, "But she's never going to get up and walk again" I snapped back.

Since I'm interested in human behaviour and I wanted to get to the root of why they did the surgery, I asked again, "Why did she have the surgery?" He didn't respond but I didn't let up. Since I had time I followed him around the ward for a few hours and kept asking him, why did she have the surgery? I worked on building the relationship and connecting with him by asking about what rods he used, what approach etc. they used in the surgery. I knew this stuff from working in the animal hospital and having helped with hundreds of orthopedic surgeries I knew the basics. I slowly got to the real reason for the surgery. As it came out, he was a young, new doctor and he needed experience. The old lady, my mother, was going to pass soon so they did the surgery for him to get experience!

I can't fully explain the rage and anger that ran thought my body but I wanted to strike out so bad at this man and the hospital. I called my older brother and told him the situation. I was so furious and enraged. I kept yelling that we are going to sue them, go to the papers, and make them pay and so on. Being older, wiser and calmer than me, he finally stated, "Rob, you have to let this go. If you chase after them and try to sue them they will drag this out in the courts and run you dry. You'll lose everything you've worked for over the last decades. You have to let this go. This isn't a battle we can win". That was a horrendous jagged pill to swallow. It made me so raw inside. I wanted to fight and get back at them. This was my mother they did this to. This was malpractice. They did a major wrong and we were in the right. But for some reason, deep from my belly brain, I knew his wisdom was correct on this matter. I had to release the poisons and let it go. Mom passed a few days later, mid-January 1999

I don't know what you would have felt or what you would have done but that was the decision we made. We didn't press charges. To this day I still think about what they did, but now, I just release the thought. I have to let that poison go. It has no purpose and serves me in no positive way. It would just be a burden to hang on to it. I've had to let it go.

Going back would I change things? I'm not sure. I try not to dwell in the past. I let it go. I've found that resentment and bitterness is like a poison you take hoping someone else gets sick. It doesn't work that way and you're the one who ends up sick! My advice would be to let go of resentment, bitterness and anger. Have more forgiveness in your heart. Forgive someone today for something they may have done to impact you. Release a toxic poison, as this can be very healing. It will lift your spirits and lighten your load as you continue to move through you life. We all need this weight removed from our shoulders. I've also found that shifting my focus to the things I'm grateful for helps speed the release of the bitterness and makes room for new positive experiences to come into my life. I'm glad I had learned such a valuable lesson from the dogs. It continues to serve me well.

Forgiveness

I hated lighting the coals for the old rusty and smelly hibachi BBQ. It was such a pain. You had to use charcoal and terrible smelling lighter fluid that often would burst into flames as you lit it. It took forever, as in forty-five minutes to heat up. However, I think it was the six months of no utilities in our house that made me the most frustrated. It was so embarrassing or "pathetic" as my mom would sometimes utter out. I couldn't bring friends around and having a girlfriend over was an absolute no way situation. The summer of 1979 was an awful time for me. Things were spiraling downwards quickly.

As I shared earlier, the mental illness my dad was experiencing was getting more severe and impacting his daily functioning more and more. He wasn't capable of holding a job in his medication induced zombie state. He hadn't been paying the bills so our utilities had been turned off for the last six months and within a few weeks, the Sheriff would be coming to round us up out of here. The BIG eviction was coming!

To this day, I don't know what exactly it was. Maybe the long shoulder length wispy hair draping from his balding head combined with his (scary) moustache, the constant shaking and undulating toe movements, the asking my friends for "butts" i.e. cigarettes, the horrendous coughing fits that went on for ten minutes or the rambling and talking to himself or even the bizarre art pieces he created and even had the nerve to put out front of the townhouse for everyone to see. I'm not sure what one thing it was, but I really felt mortified and embarrassed about my situation. And boy oh boy, was I angry at him.

I used to feel ashamed about what happened to my dad as I only looked at the situation from my point of view, the self-centered, what about poor me, point of view. I couldn't really appreciate what had happened to him and more specifically what was happening to his brain. If you break your leg and have a cast on, that's the social signal that something's wrong and it's ok to be laid up. If you have diabetes and take insulin for a biochemical dysfunction we all seem to be ok with that as well. But with mental illness, there are no overt signs; there is no cast, there is no socially recognized "biochemical dysfunctions" that we are comfortable with; you can't wear a sign. You are just weird or worse, you're "crazy". Having a father that was "crazy" with a mental illness was incredibly embarrassing to me. I was ignorant and didn't know anything about mental illness or biochemistry, I just saw the world from my point of view, he was a crazy old man, and so I blamed him.

I blamed him for all my problems and the crappy situation I was in. It was his fault I was in so much trouble with the law. It was his fault that I was such a jerk. It was his fault that we would lose our place to live, and now because of him I was out of school and had to work at a "dumb" job with a bunch of alcoholic losers. Yes, it was all HIS FAULT! I blamed him for all of it. I was angry, bitter and even hateful of this man, my father. I often thought, maybe he is doing this to me to get back at me for burning the family home down on his birthday when I was five years old. The mental torment of that event went on for years. Talk about guilt. I would think "Was this something else to punish me?" I need to share how the house fire fits into this picture and why gratitude and forgiveness is so vital to have in ones life.

The Birthday Fire

May 5th was a special day in our house. It was my sister Jane's as well as my dad's birthday. Two birthdays on one day made it a big deal. Cake, ice cream, steaks and hamburgers were going to be the order of the night. And of course, the presents. It was an exciting day.

In 1966 it seemed everyone smoked and they started early just so they didn't miss out on any of the "health" benefits and joys. Now, back then, there were no butane lighters, you had to do work to get your smoke going. It was old school times. Almost everyone used good old fashion wood matches or the newer paper matches most of which where made by the Eddie Match Company.

On this particular May 5th day in 1966 I was five and my younger brother Will who had just turned four the week before, were doing what was a fun pastime, we were playing with matches. On this windy early spring day in little town Lindsay, we were playing "War" and "shot down planes". This is when you tear off a match, put it on the striker at the bottom of the package, then with your finger on it, you swipe and flick it up into the air. It ignites then goes out with a stream of smoke billowing out from it looking like a shot down war plane. (How did a five and four year old know what a shot down warplane looked like?).

The sight of the smoking plane falling from the sky followed by the sound of the "hissss" as the plane hit the pond surface was fascinating to our little minds. But it was early spring and it was windy and a bit cold. And, like many children, we were getting bored outside so we took our game inside.

Dad designed the ranch style house we lived in with a lot of Japanese influences including the meditative indoor sitting area and the wood exterior, which was imported California redwood. This wood was quite special for the day and very special for a small town like Lindsay. It was a beautiful house both inside and outside as well. A lot of pride was in this house, our family home.

Back in those days there was very little plastic and there were no plastic bags like today. Everything was packaged in paper and the grocery bags were paper bags. My dad being an architect liked good design and our chairs were beautifully designed, sculpted if you will, works of art… made out of wood. And the garbage bag, full of paper, was sitting on the chair against the wall. There was no cheap drywall, this wall had imported wood paneling. Solid wood was the chant of the day.

Mom was in the back room sleeping with the baby, the fifth child in our family so there was no supervision for us. We were free to roam and do as we pleased. What is it that moves people, children in this case, to do things? Curiosity? Intrigue? God only knows why we did it, but we did. We started flicking matches inside the house onto the paper garbage bag.

Fifty plus year later, I can still see the bag literally burst into flames. It shocked the life out of me. It must have only taken seconds. Panic, fear and awe filled my little mind and body. At five, I knew this wasn't good. I was scared. We ran to the kitchen to get our own little colour coated red and orange metal cups, filled them with water and ran back to the burning bag. Most of the water spilled out in our haste to get the water to the fire. The few drips we put on the flames did little to slow the embers and flames from taking over the chair and wall.

After a few futile attempts we got really scared. Things were really out of control. The fire was winning this war. We knew we were going to be in deep shit. We turned and pretended it wasn't happening. We didn't go wake our mom and we didn't call 911- it didn't exist. We simply ran and went outside ignoring and hoping the problem would go away (isn't it interesting how something's never change as we get older). We left the scene and would deny it was us until later.

Mr. Mackey was a large man. He reminded me of a big strong farmer sort of man but in a suit. His good nature and kindness to us kids was so very welcome in our home. He stated he saw the smoke miles away from the school where he was picking up my older brother and sister to drive them home. And like many, he was curious to what was burning to make so much smoke. And like many, he thought it was a barn.

There is a unique sound of a car skidding on gravel. It is a grinding sound that lasts for a long time as it takes the car longer to stop. I can remember the car flying into the driveway but that's it. I have no memory of him not being able to open the door to get inside where mom and the baby were sleeping. There is no memory of the raging flames and smoke filling the sky that could be seen for tens of miles away.

The story is that he just kept shouldering the front solid wood door until he broke the lock and knocked it down. His quick action and bravery to race into the burning house filled with smoke is what saved our mom and younger baby brother. A few minutes later and it would have been over for them.

The house was gone in less than an hour. The wind fanned the flames and fueled the fire on. The fire crews ran out of water. The pump truck clogged their hoses trying to get water from the pond out back. One man was injured trying to save the lawn tractor from the carport. The police kept the crowd back. The journalist from the paper took some photos. Everyone had to just stand back and just watch it go. It went so very fast.

I stayed with the Davies family in their home downtown. The dad, Dr. Davies was our dentist. I didn't know the significance of what I did but I knew it was bad. Everyone was talking. And my name was mentioned often. The guilt stirred my guts and made me throw up over and over for days.

Being at the job site was really great for a little kid. All kinds of wood, cement mixers, weird tools, hammers, lots of nails, and the like. My dad and uncles rebuilt the house on the same foundation but this house was different. It was all brick and there were special windows and or doors in all the rooms that would allow one to escape, in case of a fire! The fire shifted how my dad practiced his craft of architecture. The fear of fire changed his designs.

May 5th 1977, my dad's and sister's birthday again but this time we are living in Toronto. We are about to have the traditional cake and ice cream when my dad makes his announcement. The same statement he made for years that contributed to my chronic guilt and shame, the spike into the deep wound of a naive and fragile five year old, "And this is the day that Robbie burnt the house down in '66". Then there was rambling about how this event ruined his life… etc.

What a crushing and killing blow to me. Did he know how deep his words impacted me? Guilt, shame and the embarrassment. The wound was deep and didn't heal. I would say it even got infected with a poison that was killing my spirit and me. It impacted how I interacted with others and how I thought of myself.

Early in the 1990's after many years of therapy this issue arose. After hearing this story, the therapist sat back, put her hand on her chin, looked off into some faraway place and was quiet for the longest of time before she shared her insight. "And thank God, no one was killed". This was the antidote to the poison that harbored in me for decades. Simple but effective. I wasn't fully cured but I felt tremendously better. The guilt was gone and the healing began.

The exact year has gone from my memory, but I clearly remember the day. May 5th, my dad's and sister Jane's birthday again. We are gathering to celebrate life, another year and to have cake and ice cream. On cue, my dad reminiscing about the past makes his striking blow of words, "And this is the day Robbie burned the house down in '66". But I was ready. I had the remedy to this blow. I simply shared the wise words from the therapist, "And thank God, no one was killed". Dad went silent. It was over. We spoke about that day's events, what everyone remembered, how lucky we all were and "And thank God, no one was killed". He let it go. Healing started to take place and everyone seemed to move on to better places.

Your Choice - Your Way

There are a few reasons I shared this story with you. Crap, shit, stuff, whatever you want to call it happens to all of us. However, it's not the events that happen to us that shape our destiny. Rather it's how we choose to respond to the event that's most important. It's how we choose to interpret the meanings we get from the event that impacts how we move forward in life. Put another way, Life is 10 percent what happens to you and 90 percent how you react to it.

It's not important to put the blame on someone or something. The important point is, an event happened and how are you going to respond to the event? What's your 90%? What meaning are you going to get from this life event? Is it going to break you, are you going to wallow in self-pity and disempowerment? Or are you going to use it as fuel to power your determination and motivation to get back up on your feet, to get back your own place again, to get to that next level in your life, to rebuild a better than before life? How is this event going to empower you? It is all your choice to make it happen.

Yes you will have crappy, down days where the world is crushing you. That's a fact, thus you will need a vision of where you are going to pull you through these days. Write down your dreams and goals in great detail and read them daily to fuel your motivation and determination. Your vision will pull you through and fuel you when you feel you can't do it on your own.

The other reason I shared this story is to impart the power of words. Be it the words we say to others or the words and stories we tell ourselves. Watch your words. They can heal and they can harm! In twenty or thirty years I hope you can look back on your life event and say, "Wow, that fire was crappy, but thank God no one died". "And look how we grew from that experience and how it made our life so much better".

You probably can't fathom this now, but you will be able to in time. Some of the "worst things" that happen to us in life end up being key milestones that give us insight, strength and skills to take our lives to that next amazing level. What story are you going to tell yourself later in your life? Using your internal strength to forgive and let go is so paramount in moving forward in life. I was learning these vital lessons from the dogs and would use them in forgiving my dad.

A Tough Pill To Swallow

Working with the dogs was helping me to develop empathy and gratitude. I'm not sure exactly when but over time I was started to wake up and realize that if I was going to blame my dad for my problems then I would also have to blame him for my success and achievements. I would have to blame him for making me so angry and miserable that I could handle the pain and burning in my legs during two hour triathlon races. It seems I could handle the pain better than most, and the anger drove me harder. The hate I felt for my life situation drove me to give up social activities to study and train my brain and body so I could get ahead and get out of that hellhole of a mess Ghetto Village. I had to get away from him and the situation as fast as I could.

This pill was going to be hard to swallow and even harder to digest. If I was going to blame him for my problems and my situation I would also have to "blame" him, by this I mean give him credit and thank him, for creating my drive and giving me the persistence to solider on when most gave up and dropped out. I would have to thank him for my motivation to get out of "Ghetto Village", the place we were living, for a better life. I would have to thank him for all my success and achievements and all the great things that are now in my life. Something seemed wrong with doing this though. It didn't sit right with me. It seems counter intuitive, almost wrong. My teen years and early twenties had been miserable. I did all the hard work to change and grow to get out of that mess, why should I give him the credit and thank him? Ah, as I learned, maturing can be tough.

My regret is, I wish he were still around so I could thank him and tell him that I forgive him and to tell him that things will be ok. The last time I saw him alive he was bed ridden and quickly dying with a failing liver in a sad and disgusting beat-up old apartment in downtown Hamilton. I drove down on a Sunday morning with his granddaughter who was five to bring him some food and to try and make amends. He had become quite disorientated with his failing health and wasn't totally with it. Today he seemed a bit agitated as well. Things started off ok, but we had a disagreement and argument. I threw the sandwiches at him and was yelling profanities as we left. I never saw him again. I hope not to have many regrets when I die, unfortunately, this will be one. I wish I were able to thank him and share my forgiveness with him. I'm trying to let this one go.

Through my studies I now understand so much more about the brain, neuro chemistry and human behaviour that I have a much greater empathy of what must have been going on in his life and how difficult it must have been for him. Having forgiveness towards someone can be very healing for your soul. I would highly recommend forgiving someone today for something that might be a stumbling block in your relationship.

Letting go can also apply to dreams or goals. I deeply wanted to become a vet and help my animal friends. I had a deep passion and a big why to do this. I tried as hard as I knew how, I studied the best I could, and I surrounded myself with smart people who could help me and mentor me. My grades were good, but not amazing, which was required for entrance to the vet program. I did all the things I knew to get there. However it wasn't to be. The circumstances were not going to allow it to happen. I had to let go of a ten-year dream I had been working towards. This was the dream that helped change the course of my life and helped me better myself. I had to let it go. I could rationalize it, make excuses as to why I didn't get into the program but I didn't. I accepted who I was and the situation I was in. I decided to move on to a new stage of my life. There was a new love in my life- biochemistry and physiology. I was thirty and it was time to make my mark in the world.

Gratitude

Understanding that life is tough, that life isn't fair and that life can be cruel allowed me to accept and understand the power of gratitude. Once I accepted this, life got easier. Life is tough so don't ask for it to be easier. Ask for guidance to get stronger and more skilled at dealing with problems. This mindset helped make me more thankful and realize how good we have it and how to be more grateful.

Being thankful leads to a great sense of gratitude, which in turn seems to make me more sensitive to others. I listen better and am more emotionally connected to them. This helps recalibrate what I pay attention to. Working on becoming other focused empowers us to be less absorbed in our own problems and more optimistic about the future.

I've learned that you can't be angry and grateful at the same time. If I chose to be thankful and grateful of what I already have in life I get into a better state, my mood improves and life just seems better. I'm happier.

Believing in my skills and myself was difficult. I found that I needed someone else to believe in me when I didn't believe in myself and thus I couldn't get to the next level in my life. Others can see the positive things in us that we often can't. Their affirming and encouraging words can be fuel for us to keep moving forward. Sometimes we do things for others that we may not normally do for ourselves.

It felt like a thousand pounds of weight on my body every morning. I couldn't move. Or more accurately, I couldn't motivate myself to move as I felt the burden of the world was on my shoulders crushing me down. My motivation battery was dead. But when I rolled over and saw them, with their big brown eyes, their tails slowly waging and sometimes the licks on my hand or face, I somehow found the energy to get up, get dressed and take them out for the morning walk. I did it for them, which it turns out, was good for me.

Over the years this consistent routine of getting up and walking them became a habit for me to get up and do something productive with the morning. If I could win the morning I could win the day. This has built a lifelong habit in me, which I'm very thankful for. It gives me time to reflect on the day and take inventory of how good I have it, the key activities I want to accomplish and it instills in me how good life can be with the simple things. It helped surface the feelings of appreciation and gratitude for life.

Take Inventory

It might sound kind of weird to you, and I know I'm not the only one who does this, however I frequently like to take inventory of where I'm at in life. I will walk through my home and do a mental inventory of the stuff, people and the environment where we live. I look in the garage and see my tools that allow me to fix and repair broken things. They also allow me to shape wood and stone to create beauty where there may not have been any before or where others couldn't see it. I see this as metaphor for my life. I see the van that we have used to take our kids on so many awesome adventures to build their appreciation of this great world. Wow, so many fun good times. I see my bikes that give me so much pleasure and help provide incredible experiences by myself or with friends. They deliver so much awesome fun.

Looking out the window at the fields and woods behind our house allows me to revel in the wonderful spot we chose to build our home. I watch the birds some of which are just passing through as they migrate up and down the North American continent thinking these are the true remnants of the dinosaur era millions of years ago and that evolution is still in play shaping the world and us even today. I've taken thousands of photos of the sunrises over the years in awe of the light show Mother Nature puts on twice a day everyday. It's always different. Amazing!

I look and see the round moon which make me realize I'm on a spinning orb travelling thousands of kilometers per second through space and the tiny atmosphere around this planet allows life to be. How mind expanding and awing!

I look over and see my wife who still laughs at my silly jokes and antics, who still makes my heart go pitter patter and who awes me with her patience and caring nature. I think about how she grew and then delivered and now nurtures our two wonderful daughters into this world. The human body is so absolutely incredible.

I think about the few strong deep relationships and social connections I've been able to forge and how lucky I am to have these people in my life. I think about the enriching conversations and shared experience we have laughing and growing as we move though life together helping each other when needed.

Each time it snows, the big plows come and clear the streets. I can ride my bike to the library and access some wonderful books, or other media. There are three large food stores close to where we live. There is so much abundance all around if I take a moment to stop and look for it. This is true for all of us! We have to look for it to see it.

I think about all those other kids who taunted me and mocked me when I was younger and I think about where they are now, how happy are they? Did they learn to have the attitude of gratitude? Did they learn how to be thankful and to have forgiveness in their hearts? Are they able to let things so they can have peace of mind and satisfaction with their life? How about you? Are you able to reflect and appreciate how good you really have it? Are you truthfully grateful for where you are at and with what you have? Are you happy with where you are?

Life will deliver us some tough blows, that's just the nature of it. But it will also impress and awe us with its abundance and beauty if we take the time to appreciate what is actually in front of and around us. Dogs taught me how to look for the good in others and myself. Open your eyes and you shall see!

We can look to others for inspiration, motivation and guidance on the ways to be more grateful and appreciative of what we have and life. Just watch the Paralympics Games or the more recent Invictus Games created by Prince Harry. I get goose bumps just thinking about them. We have nothing to complain about and besides, no one wants to hear you whine poor me! I would suggest you take inventory of where you're at with your life. If there is an area you aren't happy with, work on and build it up. Or accept where you are at and be happy with your decision. Be grateful for who you are and where you're at. Having a dog can help you get there.

I greatly enjoy starting my day walking with a dog. This simple action increases my gratitude for the day and the awe of the world and nature. It gives me time to take inventory of the good things in my life and those that are around me. In a way, it re-calibrates what I pay attention to and focus on for the day. It's setting the positive tone for my day. I ask you, what kind of day do you want to have? It's up to you and the choices you make to make it great. A day is just a day. It's what YOU make of the day that makes it great or not. Dogs taught me to not just make it through the day, rather, take as much as you can from the day and be thankful for it.

This key lesson of letting it go that I observed and learned from my dogs has served me well many times over in my life and I hope it serves you as well. Dogs don't hold grudges or resentment. They let it go. They avoid trouble. They let the pain of yesterday go. For us humans, this is something I believe we need constant reminding of.

Can you see how your life can be filled with more joy and how forgiving someone for something that may have happened in the past can reduce your burden? In how many great ways would your day be bettered if you took stock and did a quick inventory of all the wonderful people and things already in your life? And how would others feel if you shared this gratitude and positive energy with them?

Remember to take a look around and see all the abundance already in your life. What would happen if you shared some of this new positive energy with someone close to you, how would it help lift them up and make their day? How thankful for you would they be?

Learn to let things go if you want to be happy. Remember, anger is one letter away from danger! The clock is ticking and time goes by very fast. There's no point in holding a grudge or being resentful or having regrets. Let it go. Live for this day. Be grateful for the abundance that is already in your life. Be grateful and enjoy everyday with your dog.

If we stand back and look at the way dogs approach and live life we can learn some great life lessons. I know I've sure learned a lot from them. And I hope you can learn from my experiences on the ways I incorporated the lessons into my life. Dogs tend to live and focus on a simple, uncluttered life; food, fun, friends, and sleep. There is no pretense in them. They are true and authentic. What you see is what you get. Their attitude is one of curiosity with a mindset of eagerness to each and everyday. They know how to turn work into play and have fun at it. They really seem to have a deep gratitude and appreciation for where they are in life and how precious each day is. They find peace in the moment and are present to it. They seem to savior a day like a tea or coffee; nice and slow, enjoying the drink to let it warm their insides. They take as much as they can from the day instead of simply getting through the day and letting its beauty and wonders slip by.

Dogs don't carry baggage from yesterday forward; they forgive, forget and move on. They aren't caught up in wants, they just zero in on their needs. They aren't getting caught up in what other dogs are doing or what they have; they find contentment in what they have. And they sure don't need all kinds of stuff they never use. They don't build walls around their hearts to keep hurt out. And most magnificently, they give openly and freely of love. They give you and me love unconditionally. They fully trust and believe in us. Don't you agree, these dogs are the most wonderful animal companions? Thank god for our beloved dogs.

I hope this book serves you well. I hope you can obtain some sort of inspiration, motivation and guidance from the lessons I've learned and shared from my dogs. Most importantly I hope my words move you into taking full control of your life and that they help empower you to become more response-able so you can deal with any chains that are holding you back from moving forward in making your life amazing. Run to your fears and turn your troubles into treasures. I wish for you to have a more fulfilling and rewarding life with a deeper sense of purpose, happiness and satisfaction. And I hope this book gives you a different perspective on dogs, these wonderful animals that give us so much and teach us so much about living right.

A small black dog changed the trajectory of my life and helped guild me out of a deep dark rut. For this I will forever be grateful to her and other dogs in my life. JF Kennedy, in his inaugural speech spoke the words; "Ask not what your country can do for you, ask what you can do for your country". Here I would say, "Ask not what you can do for a dog, ask what a dog can do for you." I would shout my answer, LOTS!

Share The Goodness

If you have found the lessons in this book moving, uplifting or inspiring in some way, please share this book with others so they to can enjoy and benefit from the lessons we can learn from dogs.

Do You Want More?

If you have thought about applying some of the material from these lessons into your own life you can learn more on how to do this with a deeper dive, at your own pace, with **online video lessons** that I've recorded just for you. This is where you can explore more on how to apply the lessons into your life for greater meaning, purpose, fulfillment and satisfaction. This is also fun to do with other dog lovers. You can go to healthsyneryg.ca/bark and click the link to the video lessons.

Your Lessons

We all have wonderful experiences and stories from the dogs in our lives. I would love to hear about the lessons or insights you have learned from your dogs. You can share them and become part of our dog loving community at healthsynergy.ca/bark and click on the link for the blog. Don't be shy; we all want to hear how these amazing dogs have impacted your life.

Wishing you the very best of health and spirits as you travel down the path of life with a dog or two at your side.

Robert Ridpath

About The Author

Robert is a lifelong dog lover who spends as much time as possible outdoors riding his bikes and soaking up nature. He is an active cross-country skier and loves hockey. His artistic and creative flairs in gardening, stone carving and woodworking seem to be in opposition to his formal training in nutritional biochemistry and exercise physiology, but he assures us they are closely related.

Robert is a nerdy science guy who can be found at workshops and training sessions upgrading his knowledge and skills with current research in health related areas. His "real" education has come over the last 28 years dealing with many different medical professionals. He has consulted with over 1100 different clinics and doctors educating and sharing the concepts of nutritional biochemistry and functional medicine.

He is often giving talks, doing webinar trainings, or developing new ways to more simply communicate the fundamentals of health that most need and want! His current seminar series is on addressing the underlying causes of chronic illness and promoting his other book "TLC for the Body, Mind and Soul".

Robert has achieved top rankings in two sports (motocross and triathlon) and is a top master's cyclist (mountain bike). The pride of his life are his two wonderful daughters, Jenna and Jody and he is married to his longtime partner in life Heather.

You can find some of his public work on cancer prevention, stress reduction and sleep optimization through the website HealthSynergy.ca

CPSIA information can be obtained
at www.ICGtesting.com
Printed in the USA
LVHW082201231118
597942LV00009B/35/P